NUTSHELLS

Company Law

YOU'VE GOT IT
CRACKED

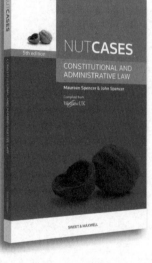
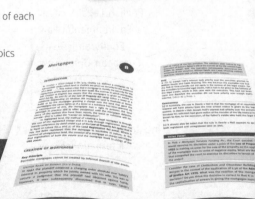

NUT**SHELLS**

Company Law

EIGHTH EDITION

by
FRANCIS ROSE
Professor of Commercial Law
University of Bristol

SWEET & MAXWELL   THOMSON REUTERS

Published in 2012 by Sweet & Maxwell
part of Thomson Reuters (Professional) UK Limited
(Registered in England and Wales, Company No. 1679046. Registered Office and address
for service: Aldgate House, 33 Aldgate High Street, London EC3N 1DL)

For further information on our products and services, visit
www.sweetandmaxwell.co.uk

Typeset by YHT Ltd
Printed in Great Britain by
Ashford Colour Press, Gosport, Hants

No natural forests were destroyed to make this product;
only farmed timber was used and re-planted

A CIP catalogue record for this book is available from the British Library.

ISBN: 978-0-41402-295-9

For Dominic

Contents

Using this Book

Welcome to our new look NUTSHELLS revision series. We have revamped and improved the existing design and layout and added new features, according to student feedback.

NEW DETAILED TABLE OF CONTENTS for easy navigation.

REDESIGNED TABLES OF CASES AND LEGISLATION for easy reference.

EXPLANATION OF KEY CASES
to highlight important information.

are the other provision.
contract of employment.

KEY CASE

CARMICHAEL V NATIONAL POWER PLC [1
Mrs Carmichael worked as a guide for
required" basis, showing groups of vi
tion. She worked some hours most w
wore a company uniform, was some
vehicle, and enjoyed many of the b
question for the court to determir
"umbrella" or "global" emplo'
·-h she worked and th

PUBLIC INTEREST DISCLO

The purpose of the Act is to protect
employers in cases where the worker '
of his employer.
        The Act protects a worker agains
or any other detriment, if the reason or
the worker has made a "protected di'

The term "worker" is given an ext'
(a) Those working under a c°
1996).
        °° workinr

**END OF BOOK REVISION
CHECKLISTS** outlining what you
should now know and understand.

NB These questions generally ı
this book. But not all of them do. I.
without looking at material discuss.

1   In which ways may persons carr
activities?
2   Distinguish between different typ
3   What are the requirements for se
4   What is a promoter? In what wa
5   What are the legal consequen'
6   What is the legal liability
induce, others to invest in lir
        In what ways can cc

NEW COLOUR CODING throughout to
help distinguish cases and legislation
from the narrative. At the first mention,
cases are highlighted in colour and
italicised and legislation is
highlighted in colour and
emboldened.

an ethnic group (∪.
psies are an ethnic group (Cr.
Rastafarians are not an ethnic grou,
ment [1993] I.R.L.R. 284)
(d) Jehovah's Witnesses are not an ethnic
Norwich City College case 1502237/97)
(e) RRA covers the Welsh (Gwynedd CC v Jon'
(f) Both the Scots and the English are covere
"national origins" but not by "ethnic or
Board v Power [1997], Boyce v British Air

It should be noted that Sikhs, Jews, Jel'
'arians are also protected on th
·nt Equality (Religion or Be''

END OF BOOK QUESTION AND ANSWER SECTION with advice on relating knowledge to examination performance, how to approach the question, how to structure the answer, the pitfalls (and how to avoid them!) and how to get the best marks.

...terials can only be
...eady learnt but where the prec...

METHOD OF ANSWERING QUESTI

There is no such thing as a perfect answer:
needs 70 per cent for a first class mark (
achieve). And, surprising as it may seem, ex
inevitably varying preferences and prejud
marking produces remarkably consistent r
The trick is to present an informed, well r
The following two sections give some
required.

ESSAY QUESTION

Example
"The rule in *Salomon v A. Salomon &*
cornerstone of English Company Law."
      Do you agree?

Preliminary
Like many essay questions, this can
should begin, however, by giving some
of your answer and to giving a balan
limited to either simply trotting o
slavish adherence to the word
    Don't begin by con

HANDY HINTS – revision and examination tips and advice relating to the subject features at the end of the book.

Planning the Answer
Different teachers may give different
varying the response depending upon
paper, although that should not make a
    It is at least sensible to jot down br
order in which they should be made (plus
lest they are forgotten). Some examiners
outline of what is to be discussed. How
particularly if the candidate is tempted ju
is waiting for his mind to start workin
soon enough. It is often best simply t
    In a problem, it is usually mo
arise in the question. Conclusio
    nly repeat what has al

Table of Cases

Table of Statutes

Introduction

METHODS OF TRADING

If he wants, an individual wishing to engage in business may operate as a sole trader, acting completely on his own account and incurring unlimited liability for his acts. More often he will wish to trade with others in a partnership. The partnership provides a suitable medium for individuals bound by mutual trust and confidence to carry on a business in common with a view of profit (Partnership Act 1890 s.1). The partners are jointly and severally liable without limit (subject to their rights of contribution and indemnity inter se) for each other's actions. This may be a discouragement to individuals who wish to invest in a business, particularly without active participation, and the limited partnership (in which the liability of "sleeping partners" is limited: Limited Partnerships Act 1907) has not become widespread. However, limited liability partnerships may now be formed (Limited Liability Partnerships Act 2000).

The practical alternative to partnership is the company, which evolved from the unincorporated association. Companies have been formed by charter or by statute but the usual method now is by registration under the Companies Acts.

COMPANIES LEGISLATION

Companies legislation has been updated and mainly consolidated in the Companies Act 2006 (hereafter CA 2006), inter alia incorporating recommendations of the Company Law Review (CLR), though leaving in force some provisions of CA 1985 and CA 1989. Except where the context otherwise requires, section references in this book are to the current form of the legislation, even during discussion of earlier cases.

Also important are reforms prompted by the Cork Report (1982) in the Insolvency Act 1985. The following year saw the consolidation of that Act and the receivership and winding-up provisions previously in the Companies Acts in the Insolvency Act 1986 (hereafter IA 1986). Certain provisions of CA 1985 were superseded by the wide-ranging Financial Services Act 1986 (FSA 1986), emanating from the Gower Reports on Investor Protection (1984 and

1985). **FSA 1986** has now been superseded by the Financial Services and Markets Act 2000 (FSMA 2000), which itself, along with **IA 1986**, has been amended by the Enterprise Act 2002. The legislation is continually amended by statutory instrument.

Further primary and secondary legislation will continue to be necessitated inter alia by Directives and Regulations under the EU harmonisation programme: e.g. the Criminal Justice Act 1993 Pt V (on insider dealing). Regulation of company law is generally the responsibility of the Secretary of State and Department for Business, Innovation and Skills ("BIS").

PUBLIC AND PRIVATE LIMITED COMPANIES

Members of an unlimited company acquire the advantage of incorporation but their personal liability to creditors of the company is unlimited. Therefore, most companies are limited companies, with the liability of the members limited to the nominal value of the shares they hold or, less commonly, the amount they guarantee to contribute to the company's liability on liquidation. A registered company is a public limited company (which words, commonly abbreviated to Plc, must follow its name) if it is limited by shares or (having a share capital) by guarantee, it offers its shares or securities to the public, and it is registered. A private limited company (whose name ends with Limited or Ltd) must not offer its securities (shares or debentures) to the public (**CA 2006 s.755**). It may re-register as a public company by passing a special resolution and inter alia if its nominal share capital is not below the authorised minimum (currently £50,000: **CA 2006 s.763**) and at least one quarter of the nominal value of each share allotted has been received. An unlimited company may re-register as a limited company (and vice versa) and a public company may re-register as a private company (**CA 2006 ss.90–96**).

REGISTRATION

For the registration of a company, delivery of certain documents to the Registrar of Companies is required (**CA 2006 s.9**). These include: the memorandum of association; statements of the company's name, situation of registered office, whether it is limited or not and its initial share structure; and the articles of association, the terms regulating the association of the members. The articles will be on the terms of model articles (such as the previously standard "Table A") prescribed by the Secretary of State, unless otherwise excluded or modified (**CA 2006 ss.18–20**). A statement of the company's registered office and the requisite particulars of the first directors and secretary plus a declaration of compliance with the requisite particulars must accompany the application.

The Registrar must satisfy himself that the statutory requirements have been fulfilled and then register the company and issue a certificate of incorporation, stating that it is incorporated and (if so) that it is a limited and a public company; the certificate is conclusive evidence of compliance with the statutory requirements and of the statements it contains (**CA 2006 s.15**). But the court may grant judicial review of a company formed for improper purposes (e.g. prostitution) and strike it off the register (*R. v Registrar of Companies Ex p. Att.-Gen.* (1980)).

....

EUROPE

A branch of a company validly registered elsewhere in the European Community is entitled to be registered though not satisfying domestic requirements (e.g. as to minimum share capital) (*Centros v Erhvers-og* (1999) ECJ).

From October 2004, existing companies within the European Union may combine to form a Societas Europaea (SE) with a presence across the borders of Member States and governed by the European Statute (Council Reg.2157/2001) and the laws of relevant Member States.

....

BUSINESS NAMES

Regulations require disclosure of the company's name in trading (**CA 2006 ss.82–85**).

Promotion

PROMOTERS

Definition

A promoter is "one who undertakes to form a company with reference to a given project and to set it going, and who takes the necessary steps to accomplish that purpose." The term has not been conclusively defined. Whether or not a person is a promoter is a question of fact. He may be anyone who participates or has an interest in setting up the company, bar someone involved in a purely professional capacity, such as a solicitor. The promoters are often the company's first directors.

The importance of establishing whether a person is a promoter lies partly in locating liability for acts done on behalf of or in connection with the company to be formed, e.g. for statements in prospectuses. (Not yet being in existence, the company cannot be liable; and promoters are not necessarily partners with each other: *Keith Spicer v Mansell* (1970)). Mainly it rests in deciding whether a person owes a promoter's fiduciary duties to the company.

Liability of Promoters

A promoter may become liable to third parties for misrepresentation or perhaps as the partner of another promoter, under agency principles in partnership law. Possibly, he will be liable to the new company under contract or conceivably for deceit or negligence (although the cases supporting the tort claims are weak). The traditional area of liability to the company is for breach of the fiduciary duties he owes to it during its promotion.

Equity will not permit him to take advantage of his privileged position in relation to the unborn company. He must make full disclosure to it, when formed, of his interest in any transaction and must not profit from his position without the company's free consent. Otherwise, he must account personally for profits made and hold on constructive trust any property received which came to him by virtue of his being a promoter.

The rule is strict because, whatever the entitlement to reward of a person whose enterprise results in the establishment of a company and the desirability of stimulating such enterprise, the promoter has an especial opportunity to divert to himself the benefits afforded to the company to be formed and to take advantage of potential investors.

Thus, a promoter who owns property before the promotion begins which he later sells to the company at a profit may retain the proceeds if he discloses all the facts. But, once promotion has begun, any property he acquires while in his fiduciary position will be held on trust for the company (subject to reimbursing him for the price) unless he clearly proves that he obtained the property solely in his personal capacity, for resale to the company on disclosing the full facts (*Omnium v Baines* (1914) per Sargant J.), although such proof might well fail if he should have obtained the property for the company directly (*cf. Keech v Sandford* (1762)). To what extent should the company be able to deny him the opportunity of profiting from the promotion?

A promoter must disclose fully the nature and extent of his interest and profit. The duty cannot be avoided by setting up a company with a board of directors which cannot and does not "exercise an independent and intelligent judgment on the transaction" and disclosing merely to that board.

KEY CASE

ERLANGER V NEW SOMBRERO (1878)

A syndicate headed by Erlanger, a French banker, acquired for £55,000 a lease of an island in the West Indies with phosphate mining rights. Erlanger then arranged for the syndicate to set up a company and to appoint its first directors, who were essentially puppets. The lease was sold, through a third party nominee, to the new company for £110,000 and, within days of the company's being established, the sale and purchase were ratified by the directors. The full details were not disclosed to members of the public who became shareholders. After the initial phosphate shipments proved unsuccessful, the true circumstances were revealed and the shareholders replaced the board of directors. It was held that the sale of the lease should be rescinded, the lease to be returned to the syndicate, which had to repay the purchase price to the company.

The directors should not contribute to disadvantaging the shareholders. Disclosure to the members would be effective if they acquiesced (*Lagunas Nitrate v Lagunas Syndicate* (1899)) but not if an undue advantage over potential investors remained, e.g. if the original members comprised or were otherwise under the influence of the promoters (*Gluckstein v Barnes* (1900)). In such a case, how long would the duty to disclose continue?

REMEDIES

The company may be able to rescind a contract entered into consequent upon non-disclosure or misrepresentation by a promoter unless one of the bars to rescission has become operative, i.e.: affirmation (unless this amounts to ratification of breach of duty by way of fraud on the minority: *Attwool v Merryweather* (1867)); lapse of time; intervening third party rights; inability to make *restitutio in integrum*; and the court's discretion to award damages in lieu of rescission (Misrepresentation Act 1967 s.2(2)).

Breach of fiduciary duty may result in liability to account and/or imposition of a constructive trust. But promoters should be able to retain expenses incurred in acquiring property in such cases (*Bagnall v Carlton* (1877)).

A slender thread of authority suggests that damages (a common law remedy) may be awarded for breach of fiduciary (equitable) duties (*Re Leeds & Hanley Theatres* (1902); *Jacobus Marler v Marler* (1913)). In principle, this is misconceived but the cases might be supported on the ground that promoters must refrain from deceit or negligence, the remedy for which is damages.

REMUNERATION AND EXPENSES

The promoter does his work and incurs expenses, by the very nature of his position, at a time before the company has become legally capable of acting. Hence, it cannot enter into a binding agreement with him to remunerate him (or even to indemnify him for expenses) nor can the company, when formed, validly ratify (i.e. retrospectively validate) such an agreement made when it did not exist (*Kelner v Baxter* (1866)). It cannot even enter into a new contract with him after formation (except under seal), for the consideration he provides will be past. The practical solution is for promoters to secure the insertion in the articles of a provision enabling the directors (amongst whom will often be numbered willing promoters) to pay promoters expenses plus reasonable remuneration, which provision will be valid if full disclosure is made (e.g. in prospectuses).

PRE-INCORPORATION CONTRACTS

Similar difficulties arise with contracts purporting to be made between the company and third parties before incorporation. At common law, the company is not normally bound by preliminary contracts. Nor will the promoter be liable for breach of implied warranty of authority (for acting as the agent of a then non-existent principal) if no implication can be made, the third party knowing the true facts. However, the company may be liable apart from contract, to pay a reasonable amount for benefits actually received, or for conversion, for refusing to permit the third party to retake goods delivered. Moreover, parties may confer rights on a company when formed, under the Contracts (Rights of Third Parties) Act 1999 s.1.

Rather than attempting to bind the company, a promoter might contract personally with a third party and forward benefits received to the company when formed, under a separate contract (subject to full disclosure). He might entitle the company on his original contract by assignment. In practice he often stipulates for his liability to cease if the company enters into an identical contract after incorporation: this is possible because, if, as usual, the third party has outstanding obligations, he will not be providing merely past consideration (*Natal Land Co. v Pauline Colliery* (1904)).

Under **CA 2006 s.51**:

> "A contract which purports to be made by or on behalf of a company at a time when the company has not been formed has effect, subject to any agreement to the contrary, as one made with the person purporting to act for the company or as agent for it, and he is personally liable on the contract accordingly."

He is also generally entitled to enforce the contract (*Braymist v Wise* (2002)). The company's agent will be personally liable whether he purports to act "on behalf of" the company or signs the contract in the company's name alone; and he may be liable though, as both parties know, the company is about to be formed and is not yet at the stage of actually being formed unless personal liability is expressly excluded (*Phonogram v Lane* (1981)). However, a person carrying on the affairs of an existing company under a new name which has not yet been registered will not be personally liable: such a company is not one that "has not been formed" (*Oshkosh B'Gosh v Dan Marbel* (1988)). Also s.51 does not impose liability on a person representing a dissolved (previously existing) company (*Cotronic v Dezonie* (1991)).

. . . .

TRADING CERTIFICATE

A public company initially registered as such cannot commence business until the Registrar receives a declaration that the nominal value of the allotted share capital meets the authorised minimum and, satisfied that it does, issues a trading certificate (**CA 2006 s.761**). This provision may be avoided by registering as a private company and converting to a public one.

Attracting Investments: Flotations

3

SHARE ISSUES AND TRANSFERS

A share is a right of ownership of a fractional part of a company's capital.

A company may issue shares by various methods. It could invite tenders or subscriptions directly from the public (usually through the agency of an issuing house of known standing). It might sell them to the issuing house, for it to resell them to the public, by issuing a prospectus or inviting subscriptions. Or it might place them with the issuing house, either for sale and resale to selected clients of the issuing house or for inviting clients to subscribe. The issuing house is rewarded, where it buys shares, by its profit on resale, and otherwise by commission, especially where it underwrites an issue (taking up itself any shares not otherwise disposed of). Any commission for underwriting an issue must be authorised by the articles and is otherwise limited to 10 per cent (**CA 2006 s.553**).

INVESTMENT SUPERVISION AND CONTROL

Trading in investment securities (shares and debentures) is generally controlled by EU Directives and national legislation and practice, as given effect by **FSMA 2000** and its subordinate legislation, and regulated by the Financial Services Agency (FSA).

No person may carry on a regulated activity unless authorised or exempted (**FSMA 2000 ss.19** and **38**). So an invitation to engage in investment activity may not be communicated in the course of a business unless made or approved by a person authorised under **FSMA 2000 s.31** (**FSMA 2000 s.21**). The FSA may grant applications to carry on activities regulated by the Act (**FSMA 2000 s.42**), e.g. carrying on an investment exchange such as the London Stock Exchange.

THE SECURITIES MARKETS

Securities may or may not be traded on an investment exchange, depending on their eligibility and the choice of the issuer. Once a company has three years of audited accounts, its securities may be listed on the Official Listed Market or "Main Market" (operated by the London Stock Exchange), thereby being freely marketable. If they are not eligible, or the issuer so chooses, the company may apply for their admission to the Alternative Investment Market (AIM).

The EC Prospectus Directive (2003/71) requires that a person making any (listed or unlisted) offer of transferable securities to the public must issue a prospectus to enable potential investors to make an informed assessment of the current position and prospects of the securities. The EC Listing Directive (2001/34) requires each EU Member State to appoint a "competent authority" to give effect to its policy of a single financial market in the EU. Inter alia, these Directives are implemented by **FSMA 2000** and its subordinate legislation: see **FSMA 2000 Pt VI ("Official Listing": ss.72–103)**. The FSA has been appointed as the UK Listing Authority (UKLA) to regulate public offerings of securities listed on the Official List of the Stock Exchange and the Authority has promulgated the governing Listing Rules. Unlisted securities are governed by the **Public Offers of Securities Regulations 1995**. Both giving effect to the Prospective Directive, the Listing Rules and the 1995 Regulations have similar effect, so the following discussion focuses on listed securities.

A prospectus for listed securities must be submitted for approval by the FSA in the form prescribed by the Listing Rules and published (**FSMA 2000 s.84**). It must include all such information as those responsible for the prospectus do or reasonably should know and which investors and their professional advisers would reasonably expect to receive (**FSMA 2000 s.80**). However, the omission from listing particulars and prospectuses for unlisted securities may be authorised if the information would seriously damage the issuer or would be contrary to the public interest and is not necessary for persons who might acquire the securities (**FSMA 2000 s.82; 1995 Regulations, reg.11**). The Listing Rules require the directors to declare that they have taken reasonable care to verify the completeness and accuracy of the information in the prospectus. A supplementary prospectus is required of significant changes to the relevant information before dealing in the securities begins (**FSMA 2000 s.81**). Approved prospectuses must be made freely available to the public and a copy sent to the Companies Registrar. Advertisements made in connection with the issue of listed securities must also be approved by the FSA (**FSMA 2000 ss.97–98**).

Any person responsible for listing particulars is liable to pay compensation to a person who has acquired securities to which they apply and suffered loss as a result of any untrue or misleading statement or omission (**FSMA 2000 s.90**). If the FSA considers that an issuer of listed securities or an applicant for listing has contravened any provision of listing rules, it may impose upon him a penalty of such amount as it considers appropriate (**FSMA 2000 s.91**).

....

IMPROPERLY ACQUIRED SHARES

If a person has acquired or continued to hold shares in contravention of a notice of objection to a person acquiring control over a United Kingdom authorised corporation or a condition imposed on the approval of the FSA, the Authority may direct in relation to specified shares that:
  (a) their transfer is void,
  (b) no voting rights are exercisable,
  (c) further shares may not be issued, and
  (d) except on liquidation, no capital or other sums is payable by the corporation in respect of them (**FSMA 2000 s.189**).

....

SUBSEQUENT DEALINGS

A subsequent purchaser of securities on a market governed by the above rules should be protected by the securities' having to comply with the rules governing the market. In addition, he will be protected by the ordinary law, especially of contract and of misrepresentation (see below).

....

CRIMINAL PENALTIES

It has been seen that **FSMA 2000** imposes criminal liability, whether to a fine and/or imprisonment, for contravention of certain of its provisions. In addition, under the Theft Act 1968 s.19, a company officer causing or contributing to publication of a statement knowing it to be false or misleading, with intent to deceive members or creditors, may be imprisoned. Those publishing false statements may also be convicted of common law conspiracy to defraud.

....

CIVIL LIABILITY

Whether on the first issue of or a subsequent dealing with shares, a person relying on a false statement may have a remedy against the company or the individual responsible (who may have to indemnify the company for liability arising from his misconduct). The following rules should be noted in addition to the above provisions of **FSMA 2000**.

A person subscribing for or purchasing shares on the basis of a misrepresentation may rescind the contract. Rescission is available against the company if it has knowledge that the contract is made on the basis of the representation, the misrepresentation is made in a prospectus deemed to be issued by the company and it is made within the authority of an agent of the company (*Lynde v Anglo-Italian Hemp* (1896)). The remedy is subject to the usual bars.

Damages for breach of contract are unlikely to be available against the company, mainly because of the rules governing the maintenance of capital and equal rights of membership, but such damages might be claimed from a transferor of shares.

A person intended to rely and actually relying on a false representation made knowingly, or without belief in its truth, or recklessly (careless of whether it be true or false) may sue for damages for deceit (*Derry v Peek* (1889)). But a purchaser of shares in the market cannot sue if the representation is made as an inducement only to original subscribers (*Peek v Gurney* (1873)) unless it is also meant to mislead subsequent purchasers or is reactivated by a later statement (*Andrews v Mockford* (1896)).

KEY CASE

SMITH NEW COURT V SCRIMGEOUR (1996)

As a result of fraud, "P" paid 82.25p for shares valued on the market at 78p. It then became known that the company itself was a victim of fraud, so that the shares were worth 44p. The general principle is that the victim should be fully compensated for all the loss directly flowing from the fraud. The prima facie measure of recovery is the price paid less the real value of the subject-matter at the date of the transaction; but that rule did not apply where the misrepresentation continued to operate after the date of the transaction so as to induce P to retain the asset or the circumstances were such that P was locked into the property. Hence, P could recover the difference between the price paid and the amount realised on re-sale.

A defendant issuing a prospectus may be liable for damages for negligence to a subsequent purchaser of the company's shares on the unlisted securities market if the defendant intended subsequent purchasers to rely on the prospectus (*Possfund Custodian Trustee v Diamond* (1996)).

A person is not debarred from obtaining compensation from a company simply by virtue of his status as a holder of, or applicant or subscriber for, shares (**CA 2006 s.655**).

A person acquiring securities on the faith of an untrue statement in listing particulars or a prospectus may claim compensation from persons responsible (above, p.10). He is, therefore, in a better position than a subsequent purchaser, who may be confined to damages for fraud (*Smith New Court v Scrimgeour*) or for negligent misstatement under *Hedley Byrne v Heller* (1964) or (so long as the defendant has contracted with him) under the **Misrepresentation Act 1967 s.2(1)**.

Damages for breach of statutory duty might be recoverable for omission of statutorily required details from prospectuses (*Re South of England Natural Gas & Petroleum* (1911)); and courts have a discretion to award compensation (deductible from damages) in criminal proceedings (**Powers of Criminal Courts (Sentencing) Act 2000 ss.130–134**).

Raising and Maintenance of Capital

4

....

RAISING FINANCE

A company may finance its activities in a number of ways. It could simply obtain an overdraft from its bank. It could buy equipment on hire-purchase terms or lease it. For borrowing of substantial sums and/or for long-term borrowing, it will often issue debentures (see Chapter 7) at a fixed rate of interest; their attraction will depend on their tax advantages and a comparison of levels of income derivable from interest and dividends on shares. An investor (especially if he controls the company) might make a capital contribution to the company, though it may be difficult to determine whether it is a loan or to be treated as a non-repayable share premium (see *Kellar v Williams* (2000) PC).

Shares provide the initial finance for most companies. Just as a company's securities may be divided into shares and debentures, so may there be ordinary shares and one or more classes of preference shares to appeal to the desires of different investors. Different classes may be created on the company's formation, but not subsequently unless in accordance with statutory procedures (**CA 2006 s.617**). Unless otherwise provided, existing shareholders have pre-emption rights on the issue of new "equity securities" (i.e., ordinary shares or rights to acquire them) (**CA 2006 ss.560–577**).

The rights of any preference shareholder are limited to the terms of issue of his class of share. Thus, if he is entitled to a fixed rate of dividend, prima facie he cannot participate in remaining income; and, if an annual dividend is not declared, only a cumulative preference shareholder can claim arrears. He may be paid off on a reduction of capital or, if his shares are redeemable, by redemption (in which case, a sum equal to their nominal value must be transferred to a capital redemption reserve) and he is not necessarily able to vote at meetings. In many respects his position is comparable with that of a debenture-holder.

....

CAPITAL

Share capital may be nominal capital (the amount of money its statement of capital and initial share holdings states that a company can raise: **CA 2006** s.10). This may comprise issued share capital (the shares actually issued) and unissued share capital. Paid up capital represents the money actually received from share issues and uncalled capital the amount still owed. Most shares today are fully paid up and often worth more than their nominal value.

Shares may be issued at a premium (for more than their nominal value); if so, the extra value must generally be transferred to a share premium account. Profits undistributed as income are kept in a reserve fund. The nominal value of his shares, therefore, indicates the maximum the member has to contribute to the company's liabilities but says nothing about the company's worth (which is better indicated by their market price), especially as fixed assets lost need not be replaced. The company's share structure could, therefore, be rationalised either by capitalising the sums in the share premium account and reserve fund and by reducing capital (see Chapter 20) or by issuing bonus shares to the existing shareholders (the issue of a bonus share, at least if accepted, is equivalent to a contract: *EIC Services v Phipps* (2003)).

RAISING CAPITAL

The liability of members of limited companies is limited to the nominal value of their shares. Certain rules help to ensure that this "creditors' guarantee fund" is not illusory. Thus, the nominal value of a public company's share capital must not be less than the authorised minimum, currently £50,000 (**CA 2006 s.763**). One quarter of the nominal value of all issued shares of a public company plus any premiums must be paid up (**CA 2006 s.586**). Shares must not be allotted at a discount (**CA 2006 s.580**), although debentures may (unless they are immediately convertible into equal value shares: *Moseley v Koffyfontein* (1904)). A commission may only be paid to underwriters if less than 10 per cent of the price and/or authorised by the articles (**CA 2006 ss.552–553**). Shares may be allotted for money or money's worth (**CA 2006 s.582**). If a public company's shares are allotted for money's worth, however, the consideration for the allotment must be valued by an expert, whose report must be made to the company and made available to the allottee (**CA 2006 s.593**).

MAINTENANCE OF CAPITAL

Prima facie, capital cannot be returned to members by the company (though, of course, they might recoup their investment by selling shares to others). Whether a transaction infringes the rule is a matter of substance, not form; thus, a sale of company assets at what a director subjectively, but mistakenly, believes to be a fair value may be valid though it transpires that it was in fact at an undervalue (*Progress Property v Moorgarth Group* (2010) SC).

In general, a company cannot acquire its own shares, a practice which would enable directors to manipulate share values, depending on the price paid for shares which the company bought (**CA 2006 ss.658–659**; see **CA 2006 ss.660–661** for shares acquired by nominees). But, if authorised by the articles, it can do so, or issue redeemable shares, redeemable out of distributable profits or the receipts from a fresh share issue made for the purpose, provided in neither case is it left only with redeemable shares (**CA 2006 ss.684–689**). A company may be liable for damages for non-performance of an undertaking to redeem shares (*British & Commonwealth Holdings v Barclays* (1995)). A company must pay in full to redeem or repurchase its own shares (*Kinlan v Crimmin*, 2006). The redemption of redeemable preference shares constitutes a reduction of capital (*Comptroller of Stamps v Ashwick* (1987) HCA).

A company must not provide financial assistance to another for the purpose of (not simply in connection with: *Dyment v Boden* (2004) CA) acquiring its or its holding company's shares unless: its principal purpose is not merely to give such assistance or to reduce liability and it acts in good faith; to distribute dividends or to allot bonus shares; or (see Chapter 20) for an authorised reduction of capital, or compromise or arrangement with creditors; it is a private company; its net assets are not reduced, unless out of distributable profits; or to employees (**CA 2006 ss.677–683**). Whether financial assistance is given must be considered in the light of the commercial realities of each transaction (*Chaston v SWP* (2002)) and may include the surrender of tax losses (*Charterhouse v Tempest* (1985)). And company A may purchase the shares of company B, even though company B's sole assets are shares in company A (*Acatos & Hutcheson v Watson* (1994)).

KEY CASE

BRADY V BRADY (1988)

"B Ltd" and its subsidiaries constituted a family business carried on in road haulage and soft drinks by two brothers. They fell out with each other, threatening the survival of the group, so they decided that each should take one of the two parts of the business and that B Ltd's assets should be divided equally between them. This involved the transfer of half of B Ltd's assets to pay off loan stock issued to buy shares in B Ltd. B Ltd was not allowed to give such financial assistance for the purchase of its own shares because, although the reason or motive was the division of the group, the plan did not have any purpose other than the acquisition of the shares.

This narrow interpretation of the purpose exception might seem to destroy it. However, in *Plaut v Steiner* (1989) there was held to be a separate (therefore justifiable) purpose of making division of the group attractive (albeit it made the company insolvent and was not, therefore, in good faith). And an agreement with the effect of providing unlawful financial assistance is not unenforceable if it could have been performed lawfully and the lender was unaware of the illegality (*Anglo Petroleum v TFB* (2007) CA).

Unless the illegal part of the transaction can be severed (*Carney v Herbert* (1984)), a prohibited loan and any guarantee of the loan (*Heald v O'Connor* (1971)) will be void (*Selangor v Cradock (No.3)* (1968)); the company and its officers may be fined; and participating directors are liable to the company for misfeasance and breach of trust (*Wallersteiner v Moir* (1974)).

However, a company which is in breach of these provisions may be able to recover losses wrongly caused to it.

KEY CASE

BELMONT FINANCE V WILLIAMS FURNITURE (1977)
The plaintiff company, through the acts of two of its directors, became the victim of a conspiracy whereby it bought property worth £60,000 (shares in a different company) from four of the defendants for the sum of £500,000, the proceeds of which were used by the four to pay £489,000 necessary to buy from the plaintiff's holding company all of the shares in the plaintiff. The plaintiff had, therefore, given financial assistance for the purchase of its own shares. Nevertheless, though (through the two of its directors) a party to the conspiracy, the plaintiff was a victim of it. Also, the statutory prohibition is for the protection of the relevant company. Therefore, the plaintiff in such a case could bring proceedings to hold fraudulent defendants liable as constructive trustees and for damages for conspiracy.

Distributions
The inevitable risk to capital in business is recognised, however. Losses to fixed assets (e.g. a mine) need not normally be made good before profits are distributed (*Lee v Neuchatel* (1889)). Losses to circulating assets (e.g. stock-in-trade) for previous accounting periods may be written off (*Re National Bank of Wales* (1899)). Distributions may normally only be made out of profits (i.e. unutilised realised profits less accumulated realised losses, so far as not previously written off: **CA 2006 s.830**) and, if a public company, provided the amount of the net assets does not become less than the aggregate of its called-up share capital and undistributable reserves (**CA 2006 s.831**). A shareholder must return an unjustifiable distribution even if he was unaware

that it was wrongful and even if he could have obtained the payment in another way, e.g. as salary or directors' fees (*It's A Wrap v Gula* (2006) CA ("family company")). Unrealised profits may be issued as bonus shares if this was authorised by the articles before December 22, 1980 (**CA 2006 s.848**). An unrealised profit on the revaluation of a fixed asset may, after provision for depreciation, be included among the realised profits (**CA 2006 s.841(5)**). An extraordinary general meeting must be called in the event of net assets falling to half of a public company's called-up share capital (**CA 2006 s.656**).

Dividends

Subject to the above and to prevailing economic restraints, dividends may be declared as provided by the articles, which generally authorise the directors to make or recommend declarations. The directors should retain sufficient profits to ensure that the company does not trade in a risky fashion and has adequate reserves for its business. But the shareholders have a legitimate expectation of receiving dividends where a company is trading profitably so, even if profits are not being accumulated other than for their benefit, a member is entitled to realise her interest in the business by petitioning for winding-up on the "just and equitable" ground (*Re A Company (No.00370 of 1987) Ex p. Glossop* (1988)). Members are prima facie entitled to participate equally in dividends and can sue for them once declared. Although distributions may not be made in the absence of profits, a preference shareholder whose shares entitle him to dividends regardless of declaration may prove for arrears on liquidation (*Re New Chinese Antimony* (1916)).

Shares

5

BECOMING A SHAREHOLDER

A person may become a shareholder by subscribing to the memorandum and having one or more shares allotted to him, or by having shares transferred to him by an existing shareholder, or by applying for shares and having them allotted to him (generally in response to a prospectus). An allottee has a contractual right to be registered which, under a renounceable letter of allotment, he can renounce (assign) in favour of a third party (who pays him for it). Membership is generally signified by registration (*Envirico v Farstad* (2011)).

REGISTRATION

Companies must keep a register of the class and extent of members' shareholdings, which is open to inspection and is prima facie evidence of the details therein (**CA 2006 ss.112–128**). A member may hold shares or a pro- portion of stock (into which paid-up shares may be converted). But a shareholder with a share warrant (a negotiable instrument, transferable by delivery and carrying a right to a certain number of shares: **CA 2006 s.779**) is not normally considered to be a member and is not entered as such on the register (**CA 2006 s.122**). Shares are "issued" on registration (*National Westminster v I.R.C.* (1994)).

The acquisition and disposal of major shareholdings must be disclosed (FSA Handbook (**Disclosure Rules and Transparency Rules**, DTR; **CA 1985 s.444**), dealings in and the exercise of rights under which may be restricted for non-compliance (**CA 1985 ss.454–457**).

EFFECTS OF SHAREHOLDING

A share is an item of property and normally freely transferable (*Stothers v William Seward (Holdings)* (1993)). It gives its holder an interest in the company measured by a sum of money (representing the prima facie extent of his liability to creditors) and entitling him to the rights contained in the articles (which rights may be varied, diluted or redenominated: **CA 2006 s.617**). The value of shares is generally their market price (*Short v Treasury Commissioners* (1948)), although a large number whose votes confer control may be worth more.

PREFERENCE SHARES

Prima facie, shareholders have equal rights but a company can alter its articles to issue another class of shares carrying preferential rights (*Andrews v Gas Meter* (1897)), in which case a presumption of equality applies to those aspects where there is no preference (e.g. a right to a preferential dividend does not exclude the right to equal participation in capital on liquidation: *Birch v Cropper* (1889)).

A preference which does exist is deemed to be exhaustive: so a member entitled to a preferential dividend may not participate in the remaining profits (*Will v United Lankat* (1913)) and one entitled on liquidation to a return of capital subscribed may not participate in remaining assets (*Scottish Insurance v Wilsons & Clyde* (1949)). Moreover, undistributed profits which are capitalised are treated on liquidation as capital and not as undistributed dividends (*Dimbula v Laurie* (1961)). Where preference shareholders not entitled to participate in surplus assets on winding-up are paid off because of a reduction in capital, their only entitlement is to the nominal, not the market, value of their shares (*Re Chatterley-Whitfield* (1949)).

CALLS AND LIENS

The nominal value of a share specifies the maximum liability of a member of the company (and ultimately to its creditors). A share in a public company must be paid up by at least 25 per cent (**CA 2006 s.586(1)**) and the company can make calls on the holder up to the unpaid value. The articles may give the company a lien over the share for calls on the holder up to the unpaid value. They often empower it to forfeit the share for unpaid calls. Problems are rare since most shares are fully paid up.

A lien is an equitable charge on the share. It becomes effective on a specified event (e.g. for calls, immediately shares are issued). Thus, a different equitable interest of which the company has notice overrides a lien for debts due from the member (which it could set off against dividends) if the member only becomes indebted after the interest arose (*Bradford Banking v Briggs* (1886)). Once a lien does become effective, it binds a third party acquiring a later equitable interest, as he has constructive notice of the articles giving the lien.

. . . .

SHARE CERTIFICATES

Under **CA 2006 s.769**, a company must within two months of the allotment of shares or debentures or within two months of the lodging of a transfer of such securities, complete certificates, unless:

(a) it is otherwise provided in their original issue;
(b) the allotment is to, or the lodging of transfer is with, a Stock Exchange nominee; or
(c) it is excused under the Uncertificated Securities Regulations 2001 (by electronic communication with CREST).

A share certificate is prima facie evidence that the person therein named was at the time of issue a shareholder and registered as such (**CA 2006 s.68**) and the company is estopped from denying its statement as against a person relying on it (who might be able to recover damages if the statement were untrue: *Re Bahia Railway* (1868)). Thus, a company cannot make calls on shares it certifies as fully paid up (*Burkinshaw v Nicolls* (1878)).

KEY CASE

RE BAHIA RAILWAY
Two rogues obtained a forged transfer to themselves of a woman's shares. They lodged the transfer and her share certificate with the company, which registered them as owners and issued a new share certificate to them. Relying on the new certificate, the plaintiffs bought the shares on the Stock Exchange and were duly registered by the company, which issued them with a new share certificate. The original forgery came to light and the original owner had her name substituted on the register for those of the plaintiffs. However, the company had issued the fresh share certificate to the rogues with the intention that it could be relied upon in the market by purchasers of the shares. The company was, therefore, estopped from denying its truth and, although the plaintiffs were not entitled to remain registered as shareholders, they could recover from the company for the loss of the shares based upon their value at the time from which the company refused to recognise them as shareholders.

The estoppel may be available to the person to whom the certificate is issued as well as to subsequent parties (*Balkis v Tomkinson* (1893)). But it will not avail a person who has not relied on the representation or who has put forward a forged transfer to the company (*Simm v Anglo-American Telegraph* (1879)). Where a person, even if innocent, submits a forged or fraudulent share transfer for registration and receives a new share certificate which he transfers to a third party who subsequently claims damages from the company, he must indemnify the company (*Royal Bank of Scotland v Sandstone*, 1998), yet not if it was genuine but inaccurate (*Cadbury Schweppes v Halifax* (2006)).

If the share certificate itself is forged, it does not constitute any representation by which the company can be bound. It is a nullity and cannot be relied upon by a person so as to give him rights against the company for its turning out to be untrue (*Ruben v Great Fingall Consolidated* (1906)).

TRANSFER AND TRANSMISSION OF SECURITIES

Formal documentation has traditionally been necessary for the transfer of shares, although the Secretary of State is now authorised to provide by regulation for title to securities to be evidenced and transferred without a written instrument (**CA 2006 ss.783–790**): see the Uncertificated Securities Regulations 2001. Shares may normally be transferred, and the transfer should be registered; either with the Companies Registrar; or—more commonly now that dematerialised (uncertificated) shares may be simultaneously transferred and registered by the computer operator CREST—with CREST (and recorded by the company) or with the company, in either case also with notification to the Registrar.

However, the articles may restrict transfer, in which case a refusal to register must be made within two months of its being lodged (**CA 2006 s.770**) and must not be made in bad faith.

KEY CASE

RE SMITH & FAWCETT (1942)
The company had two directors and shareholders, Smith and Fawcett, each with 4,001 shares. The articles gave the directors an absolute discretion to refuse registration of any share transfer. Fawcett died. Smith and a new co-opted director refused to register the transfer of the deceased's shares into the names of any of his executors, though Smith offered to register 2,001 of the shares and himself to purchase the remaining 2,000. The plaintiff executor's application to the court for

A restriction in the articles on transfer of shares, e.g. conferring a right of pre-emption on existing shareholders (which makes a transfer ineffective until a reasonable opportunity has been given to enable exercise of the right: *Tett v Phoenix* (1985)) may prima facie only cover transfer of the legal, and not also the beneficial, interest (*Safeguard v National Westminster Bank* (1981)). Normally, shares are transferred by sale, in which case the transferor's liability to the transferee depends on contractual principles.

The seller should transfer his share certificate to the buyer so that the company will readily consent to registering him as a member. If the seller only transfers part of his holding, he should deposit his share certificate with the Stock Exchange (for quoted shares) or the company, which will issue a certificate of transfer, stating that a share certificate covering the relevant shares has been deposited (*George Whitechurch v Cavanagh* (1902)). It does not necessarily represent that there has been a transfer or that the transferee is entitled to the shares (*Bishop v Balkis* (1890)). It operates as a representation by the company to a person acting on it that documents have been produced to it showing the transferor's *prima facie* title to the securities specified, but not as a representation that the transferor has any title to them (**CA 2006, s.775**).

Fully-paid registered securities may be transferred by a stock transfer form approved under the **Stock Transfer Act 1963**. For a transfer to be registered by the company, an instrument of transfer must be delivered to the company (**CA 2006 s.770**), by either the transferor or transferee. The transferor does not guarantee registration, in the absence of which he holds the shares on trust for the transferee (*Hardoon v Belilios* (1901)). A person presenting a forged transfer must indemnify the company for loss it suffers (*Welch v Bank of England* (1955)). If the register is altered in consequence, the true shareholder may be reinstated and compensated for loss suffered (*Barton v L.N.W.R.* (1889)).

An unregistered transferee, having only an equitable interest, takes subject to other equitable interests of which he has notice when he acquires his interest. But, if equitable interests are equal, the first to register, and to acquire the legal interest, prevails (*Shropshire Union v R.* (1875)). Otherwise, the first in time has priority, unless a subsequent claimant acquires a right against the company to be registered before it receives notice of a further claim (*Peat v Clayton* (1906)).

Title to shares is decided by the law of the place where the shares are situated; under English law this is the place where the company is incorporated (*Macmillan v Bishopsgate Investment Trust (No.3)* (1995)).

Market Abuse

6

THE PROBLEM

Controversy has been generated over the use of confidential information affecting the value of securities which is taken into account by the person in possession of it in deciding whether to buy or sell shares, so as to make a future profit or avoid an impending loss. The ability to do this has been defended as the entrepreneur's just reward and as helping the price of securities to reflect their true worth. More often, "insider trading" or "insider dealing" is seen to be commercially immoral, as giving the insider an unfair advantage over other investors. How can it be prevented?

One possibility is to require disclosure of such information. But the insider may be under a confidential duty not to disclose (see *Percival v Wright*, below). If he had to disclose, should he do so only to the person with whom he is dealing or to the public in general? And is merely requiring disclosure sufficient for the other party without an additional remedy?

A further possibility is to enable the "outsider" to rescind the contract. Another is to try to eliminate the profit motive by making an insider account for his unfair profit. But to whom? If to the company, the company may resolve not to call him to account. If it did and he were a member, he would derive some benefit anyway. But the company may have suffered no loss, and accounting to the company would not compensate the outsider, who would be difficult to identify if it were an anonymous Stock Exchange transaction. Moreover, whatever remedy an outsider were to seek, he might find it difficult to prove to what extent, if any, the use of the inside information affected the transaction. And should an outsider who dealt with an insider be in a better position than one who dealt with another person not in possession of such information?

Some have argued that the only real deterrent is to impose criminal liability for insider dealing, a method which could unfortunately ban legitimate dealings where there was no abuse of the inside information, by persons who are after all dealing with their own securities. It could also discourage persons who at present freely co-operate in BIS investigations but who would not wish to run the risk of implication—so how could the criminal penalties be enforced?

Is then a better solution self-restraint and self-regulation? The Stock

Exchange rules and the disciplinary powers of the Exchange and the Takeover Panel may go a long way to alleviating the problem. But they do not give an individual locus standi to enforce the rules, nor do they help an outsider not dealing in the market. Similarly, administrative control by the Secretary of State is arguably of little use to individuals and may be thought ineffective without adequate supportive criminal sanctions.

FSA MODEL CODE FOR SECURITIES TRANSACTIONS BY DIRECTORS OF LISTED COMPANIES

This Code obliges listed companies to require persons discharging managerial responsibilities (PDMRs) to ensure that they and employees with access to information do not deal in the company's securities without prior clearance, which clearance should not be given for specified periods. However, the duties imposed by the Code are owed to the FSA by the company, not to a share purchaser by the director (*Chase Manhattan Equities v Goodman* (1990)), against whom the sanction is blacklisting by the Stock Exchange or possibly disqualification under the Company Directors Disqualification Act 1986 (see below pp.66–71).

THE COMMON LAW

The common law position is based on *Percival v Wright* (1902).

KEY CASE

PERCIVAL V WRIGHT (1902).
Shareholders offered to sell shares to directors who knew their true value was greater because of an impending take-over bid, which information their confidential obligations to the company forbade them to disclose. For that reason it was decided that the shareholders could not rescind the contract. The directors had no general duty to the shareholders to disclose price-sensitive information to them.

(Likewise, directors of a trust company do not owe duties to the beneficiaries of the trust: *Gregson v HAE Trustees* (2008)). In New Zealand, in *Coleman v Myers* (1977), a director was liable to shareholders in a small family company where a fiduciary duty to them arose because of the special relationship. The United States courts have generally circumvented the decision by extending the categories of "special circumstances" requiring disclosure. Not so for the

English courts, although it was held in *Allen v Hyatt* (1914) that directors exercising options to buy members' shares granted prior to a merger should account to those members for profits made, since in negotiating the sale of the shares to the take-over bidder they were acting as the members' agents.

THE CRIMINAL JUSTICE ACT 1993 PART V

The Criminal Justice Act 1993 Pt V reformed the law (inter alia by implementing the EC Directive on Insider Dealing (1989); now superseded by the Market Abuse Directive (2003)) as follows.

If an individual knowingly has information which is "insider information" (i.e. non-public, specific, price-sensitive information about particular securities: **s.56**) and he has that information as an "insider" (i.e. knowingly, being a director, employee or shareholder or an issuer of securities, or through access by virtue of his employment, office or profession: **s.57**), then, whatever his general intention (*Spector Photo Group v CBFA* (2009) ECJ), he commits an offence if (**s.52**):

(i)   where the relevant acquisition or disposal occurs on a regulated market, or where he acts as or relies on a professional intermediary, he "deals" (i.e. acquires or disposes, or procures the acquisition or disposal of: **s.55**) price-affected securities; or

(ii)   he encourages another person to deal in such securities, knowing or having reasonable cause to believe that the acquisition or disposition occurs on a regulated market, or that the person dealing acts as or relies on a professional intermediary; or

(iii) he discloses the information to another person other than in the proper performance of his employment, office or profession.

The offence is punishable by a fine and/or up to seven years' imprisonment (**s.61**). No contract is made void or unenforceable under the Act (**s.63**) but it may be held unenforceable at common law (*Chase Manhattan v Goodman*, (1990)).

Under **s.53**, the accused may prove the following defences.

To a charge of dealing or encouraging dealing ((i) and (ii) above), he may plead that:

(a)   he did not expect the dealing to result in a profit attributable to the fact that the information was price-sensitive; or

(b)   he believed on reasonable grounds that the information had been disclosed sufficiently widely to ensure that no-one participating in the dealing would be prejudiced by not having the information; or

(c) he would have done what he did even if he did not have the information.

To a charge of disclosure ((iii) above), he may plead:
(a) that he did not expect any person, because of the disclosure, to deal in securities on a regulated market, or by acting as or relying on a professional intermediary; or
(b) though he had such an expectation, that he did not expect the dealing to result in a profit attributable to the fact that the inside information was price-sensitive.

It is, however, no defence that the accused obtained the information without having actively sought it (*cf. Att-Gen's Reference: No.1 of 1988* (1989)).

The Act makes various provisions regarding information obtained by or from such individuals and Crown servants, relating to a first or associated company, and covering market and off-market dealings.

If the Secretary of State believes that there may have been a contravention of CJA 1993 Pt V, he may appoint inspectors to investigate (**FSMA 2000 s.168**) and they may obtain a search warrant to assist entry (**FSMA 2000 s.168**). Unlawful non-co-operation with these investigations is a criminal offence (**FSMA 2000 s.177**; *Re an Inquiry under the Company Securities (Insider Dealing) Act 1985 (Warner's Case)* (1987)).

THE FINANCIAL SERVICES AND MARKETS ACT 2000

FSMA 2000 s.118 defines as market abuse behaviour which fails to comply with reasonable market standards in relation to qualifying investments, based on generally unavailable information relevant to investment transactions, which distorts the market and is likely to give a market user a false impression about investments. Market abuse may be avoided by compliance with the code of market conduct issued by the FSA (**FSMA 2000 ss.119–122**). If there is market abuse, a penalty may be imposed by the FSA or the court (**FSMA 2000 ss.122 and 129**). The court may, on application by the FSA, make an order restraining market abuse (**FSMA 2000 ss.380–381**) and, on application by the FSA or the Secretary of State, make an order requiring restitution (**FSMA 2000 s.382–383**). The FSA may itself make restitution orders against authorised persons (**FSMA 2000 s.384**).

Moreover, it is an offence: knowingly or recklessly to make a misleading, false or deceptive statement, promise or forecast, or dishonestly to conceal material facts, with a view to inducing or deterring an investment agreement (**FSMA 2000 s.397(1)–(2)**); or to create a false or misleading impression as to the market in or price of investments to induce a person to deal or refrain from dealing in them (**FSMA 2000 s.397(3)**).

Borrowing: Debentures and Charges

7

DEBENTURES

A company may raise finance by borrowing as well as by issuing shares. This is commonly done on a long-term basis by means of debentures, documents evidencing the amount of the debts. Instead of a series of debentures for a number of separate debts, it may create one fund of debenture stock and issue certificates for particular divisions of the fund. In many ways, a debenture-holder is as much an investor as a shareholder. But a shareholder is a member of the company, whereas a debenture-holder is a creditor, whatever the similarities or dissimilarities between the rights and obligations of the two.

The law governing the transfer of the securities held by share-holders and debenture-holders is basically similar, apart from the fact that debentures must be transferred as a whole (therefore there is no need to certify transfers of them) and are generally transferable without limitation (bearer debentures are negotiable instruments). In other respects, the law differs.

RIGHTS OF DEBENTURE-HOLDERS

Whereas the articles of association can be varied, the rights of debenture-holders are fixed by the contract of loan and any attempted variation of them by the company (other than under a compromise or arrangement) will be a breach of contract. Hence, although the articles of association are alterable by statute, so that an alteration cannot be restrained by injunction (*Punt v Symons* (1903)), a declaration may be granted that an alteration of articles on which the debenture contract is based is nevertheless a breach of that contract (*Baily v British Equitable Assurance* (1904)). And (though a shareholder generally has to accept an alteration under **CA 2006 s.21**) the court might exercise its discretion to grant to a debenture-holder an injunction to restrain the company from acting according to the articles as altered (e.g. if such action would weaken his position by putting the company's capital at risk). If the breach of contract were sufficiently serious, the debenture-holder might be justified in terminating his contract with the company and claiming repayment of his investment plus interest.

In these cases, a debenture-holder can bring a debenture-holder's action on behalf of the debenture-holders (the rule in *Foss v Harbottle*, below p.89, only applies to shareholders). But these remedies are only necessary for holders of unsecured ("naked") debentures. More often, debentures will be issued so as to give their holders the improved remedies provided by some form of security.

CHARGES

Any form of security interest (fixed or floating), other than an interest arising by operation of law, is for the purposes of **CA 2006 Pt 25** (registration of charges), known as a charge. Classification as a charge is a matter of substance not form.

> ### KEY CASE
>
> RE CURTAIN DREAM (1990)
> Churchill agreed to extend credit to "CD", and CD agreed to sell its stock to Churchill for sale back to CD, reserving title to Churchill until payment. The arrangement was held to create a charge over CD's goods (which was void for non-registration).

Classification of a charge as fixed or floating (important for priority) depends upon (a) the parties' intentions and (b) not the nature of the assets but (c) the company's freedom to use them in the ordinary course of business (*Agnew v IRC* (2001) NZPC; *Re Spectrum Plus* (2005) HL). If the company needs managerial control of fluctuating assets, the charge cannot be fixed (*Smith v Bridgend CBC* (2001)).

Fixed Charges
One possibility is for the company to create a fixed charge over certain of its property for the amount of the loan. This is reasonably simple in respect of certain forms of property (e.g. a mortgage of buildings), though it may apply to any, even a future, asset if the company's freedom to dispose of it is excluded. But fixed charges are inappropriate for fluctuating assets (e.g. raw materials and finished products), which may constitute a large part of the company's assets (and so a major means of providing security) but which the company must be able to transfer freely and with unencumbered title if it is to carry on business efficiently. The difficulty has been overcome by the invention of the floating charge.

Floating Charges

A floating charge floats over the whole or a part of the company's assets, which may fluctuate as disposals and acquisitions are made free of the charge. The traditional theories are: (1) that the lender has a current charge and licenses the company to deal with the property freely until crystallisation; or (2) that it is a mortgage of future assets, i.e. a right to have a charge on the assets actually in the hands of the company at crystallisation. A different analysis is (3) that it is a fixed charge subject to defeasance (by the chargor's permitted dealing with charged assets).

The charge crystallises on the occurrence of a specified event (automatically on a winding-up), in which case it becomes a fixed charge over assets then in the company's possession. Its value as security then depends, of course, on the assets remaining in the company's possession, so it is not uncommonly provided that a receiver may be appointed in certain circumstances to safeguard the interests of debenture-holders if they are at risk. This is usually done by trustees for debenture-holders, in whom legal title to debentures is commonly vested so that there is one small body which can exercise rights on behalf of a variety of debenture-holders. The contract may provide for automatic crystallisation, e.g. allowing the chargee by giving notice to convert a floating into a fixed charge and thereby to acquire priority over preferential creditors (*Re Brightlife* (1986)).

The Secretary of State may make regulations: requiring notice to be given to the Registrar of the occurrence of events affecting the nature of the security under a registered floating charge (e.g. automatic crystallisation) and the exercise of powers under registered charges; and limiting the ineffectiveness of such charges for non-compliance with the regulations (**CA 2006 s.860**).

Registration of Charges

A registrable charge must be registered within 21 days of its creation or the acquisition of property subject to it (**CA 2006 ss.860–877**). Registration may be effected by any interested person. The Registrar must keep for each company a register of charges on property of the company containing the particulars and other information delivered to him; and any person may require the Registrar to provide a certificate stating the date on which any specified particulars of, or other information relating to, a charge were delivered to him (**CA 2006 s.863**).

The Registrar's decision to register a charge (and possibly on other matters) is subject to judicial review and may be quashed for error of law, but this is unlikely to occur.

R. v Registrar of Companies ex p. Central Bank of India (1985)
The chargee applied in February, on an incomplete statutory form and presenting copies of the relevant documents rather than the original instrument creating the charge required by the statute, for registration of a charge. In March, a petition was presented for winding-up and, in August, on further representations by the chargee, the charge was registered. It was held at first instance that the applicant bank, as one of the company's unsecured creditors, had locus standi to apply for judicial review of the Registrar's decision to register the charge and to issue a certificate of registration. The Court of Appeal considered that registry of the charge in default of delivery of the original documents by which it was created or evidenced was an error of law. However, the then applicable legislation provided that the certificate is conclusive evidence that the statutory requirements as to registration had been satisfied (see below, p.35). Therefore, the Court of Appeal found itself precluded from considering evidence adduced to show non-compliance with the registration requirements. Accordingly, it allowed the Registrar's appeal from an order quashing the registration.

The company and any officer at fault may be fined for non-registration (**CA 2006 s.860**). The court has a discretion to extend the registration period (**CA 1985 s.873**), which can be exercised even though liquidation is imminent (*Re Braemar Investments* (1988)). However, a first chargee who registers late will not get priority over a registered second charge unless it was created within 21 days of the first (*Watson v Duff* (1974)).

The **Companies Act 2006 s.860**, lists the registrable charges, including those on land, on goods, on intangible movable property (e.g. intellectual property and book debts), for securing issues of debentures, and floating charges. Not every charge is registrable. Payment of money into a special account on trust to pay the company's debts is not (*Carreras v Freeman* (1984)). But an equitable charge on land resulting from the deposit of title deeds is, because, though it is created by presumption of law, it is contractual in nature (*Re Wallis Simmonds* (1974)). Similarly an unpaid vendor's lien is not, being a creation of law and not arising from contract (*London & Cheshire Ins. v Laplagrene* (1970)); but, though an agent's liability to account arises by (agency) law, a supplier's right to the proceeds of goods delivered to a company under a retention of title clause as agent is created by contract, and so is registrable (*Tatung v Galex* (1988)). A charge over a creditor's right to payment by the chargee (a "charge-back") is registrable (*Re BCCI (No.8)* (1997), per HL).

KEY CASE

WELSH DEVELOPMENT AGENCY V EXPORT FINANCE [EXFINCO] (1991)
"E" provided finance to "P Ltd". They agreed that goods to be supplied
by P to its customers would first be sold to E then resold to the customers by P as agent for E (as undisclosed principal). "W" had a
floating charge over P's assets. It was held that E acquired an interest
in P's manufactured products by transfer of title under a contract of
sale and not by way of an unregistered charge over assets still
belonging to P.

Retention of Title Clauses

Where a supplier delivers goods to the company under a retention of title
clause, on the basis that legal and equitable ownership remain in the supplier and that the goods (whether in the same or modified form) may be sold
by the company as the supplier's agent, the restriction is not registrable as
the goods do not become the property of the company and the restriction is
not created by it (*Aluminium v Romalpa* (1976); *Borden v Scottish Timber*
(1979)). By this means, suppliers can secure themselves (for the price of the
goods supplied and even for all other liabilities owed to them by the company: *Armour v Thyssen* (1990)) and deprive the company of assets which
may become subject to an existing floating charge. A receiver dealing with
the goods as the company's property will be liable for conversion (*Clough
Mill v Martin* (1984)).

   Whether a company acquires goods subject to a retention of title
clause or creates a charge over its own goods is a matter of substance, not
form (*Re Curtain Dream*, above, p.31). Where the supplier under a retention of
title clause retains only the beneficial title, this has been held to amount to
the creation by the receiving company of a registrable equitable floating
charge (*Re Bond Worth* (1979), although the decision may be wrong: *cf. Abbey
National v Cann* (1990)). Similarly, a company receiving goods under a contract whereby the supplier is to acquire rights over their product when mixed
with other goods (whether the latter goods belong originally to the company
or to a third party) is creating a floating charge over the product, which charge
requires registration (*Borden v Scottish Timber* (1979); *Re Peachdart* (1983)).
A repairer's stipulation that he obtains ownership of an article of a company
into which he incorporates parts as security for his costs also constitutes a
registrable charge over the company's assets (*Specialist Plant Services v
Braithwaite* (1986)).

Effects of Non-registration

Where a registrable charge created by the company is not registered, the security is void against an administrator or liquidator of the company and any person who for value acquires an interest in or right over property subject to the charge where the beginning of insolvency proceedings or acquisition occurs after the charge's creation (CA 2006 s.874). Thus, a later chargee may register his charge and gain priority over an unregistered earlier charge of which he is aware (*Re Monolithic* (1915)). The unregistered chargee may still enforce his security against the company; moreover, on failure to register, the company becomes liable to repay him his loan immediately (CA 2006 s.874(3)). A charge over land which is registered according to CA 2006 may or may not also be registered with the Land Registry or Land Charges Registry to be fully effective (*Property Discount Corp v Lyon* (1980)).

Where the registered particulars are not complete or accurate, the charge is void, unless the court orders otherwise (because such non-registration has not been prejudicial), against an administrator or liquidator of the company or (unless he acquires it subject to the charge: **CA 2006 s.405**) against a person acquiring an interest in or right over its property (**CA 2006 s.874**). A charge will not be void as against a subsequent charge unless the latter is registered within 21 days of its creation, or before registration of full and complete particulars of the earlier charge, or so far as rights are disclosed by incomplete and inaccurate registered particulars of the later charge.

Effects of Registration

The Registrar's certificate is conclusive evidence of compliance with the statutory registration requirements (**CA 2006 s.869**). The certificate is not conclusive as to other matters. However, if registered in compliance with the statutory requirements, the charge is valid according to the terms of its creation, even though all the details have not been registered. Registration constitutes constructive notice of the existence of a charge but not necessarily of its contents. Thus, a subsequent chargee is unaffected by an unregistered restriction on the creation of subsequent charges (*Wilson v Kelland* (1910)).

Administration Orders

From presentation of a petition for an administration order (below, pp.74–75) until the order's expiry or 12 months after it is made, charges cannot be enforced, or goods supplied under retention of title clauses repossessed, except with the court's leave before the order is made (**IA 1986 ss.10–11**).

Reform

The system of registration of charges was criticised by Diamond's Department of Trade consultative paper in 1986, which suggested that there should be a uniform system for registering all securities other than land. Currently, the Law Commission has recommended replacement of the current system of registration with one for electronic notice-filing for company charges (Law Com No.296 (2005)).

Priorities of Charges

A registered charge in general gives the chargee a prior right, according to its terms, over a subsequent charge and any previous unregistered charge. But a subsequent floating charge can be created over a particular part of the assets covered by a previous floating charge over the wider category (*Re Automatic Bottle Makers* (1926)). And a later fixed charge will gain priority over a previous floating charge covering the assets in question (*Government Stock v Manila Ry* (1896)). In either case, this is because floating charges are created with knowledge of the possibility of subsequent dealings with assets.

On crystallisation, a floating chargee can only enforce his security over property which is not otherwise subject to existing rights. Thus, a debtor of the company can maintain a right of set-off which he has at the time of crystallisation (*Biggerstaff v Rowatt's Wharf* (1896)) but not one he acquires after the chargee's rights have crystallised (*Robbie v Witney* (1963)).

An existing registered charge, even if it prohibits the creation of subsequent charges, will not have priority over a charge already existing over after-acquired property, or created in order to acquire it (e.g. to secure payment of purchase moneys), for the property might not otherwise have been acquired (*Security Trust v Royal Bank of Canada* (1976)).

Unregistered chargees may prove in a company's liquidation as unsecured creditors and rank in priority as such. Fixed chargees can simply enforce their security according to the terms of the charge. The rights of floating chargees are, however, postponed to those entitled to preferential payments on a winding-up (**IA 1986 s.175(2)(b)**) and to the unsecured creditors' fund (**IA 1986 s.176A**; below, p.105). A floating charge created within 12 months of the onset of insolvency (24 months if in favour of a person connected with the company) or between the presentation of a petition for and the consequent making of an administration order is, unless the chargee was not connected with the company and the company was solvent immediately after its creation, void except to the amount of any consideration provided simultaneously with or subsequently to its creation, plus interest (**IA 1986 s.245**).

The charge may be attacked as a fraudulent preference if redeemed within six months of liquidation (*Re Parke's Garage* (1929)) but the invalidity

of the charge does not otherwise affect the validity of the underlying debt or
its discharge (ibid.) or the appointment and acts of a receiver under the terms
of the charge prior to liquidation (*Mace Builders v Lunn* (1986)).

KEY CASE

MACE BUILDERS V LUNN (1986)
In May 1981, the company granted to the defendant (its managing
director) a floating charge to secure its indebtedness to him up to
£100,000. Since the company failed to make repayments, in November
1981, the defendant exercised his right under the debenture to appoint
himself receiver. As such, he sold the assets covered by the charge,
applying the proceeds in repayment of the debt owed to him by the
company. In May 1982, the company went into liquidation. The liquidator asserted that the charge was invalid as having been created
within the statutorily proscribed period immediately preceding insolvency (under a predecessor of IA 1986 s.245, above). Nevertheless, it
was held that the section did not affect the validity of anything done
under the authority of the charge before the actual commencement of
the winding-up.

Corporate Personality

8

SEPARATE LEGAL PERSONALITY

One of the consequences of forming and incorporating a registered limited liability company is that the members create a body which is recognised as having an independent legal personality. A registered limited liability company, whether created under English or foreign law (*Arab Monetary Fund v Hashim (No.3)* (1991)), is recognised in law as a person, with capacity to act as such, although of course not necessarily in the same way that a natural person can act. Moreover, the company's personality is distinct from that of each and all of its members, albeit there may be similarities.

Salomon's Case

KEY CASE

SALOMON V SALOMON (1897)
The leading case is *Salomon v Salomon* (1897). Salomon formed a company with 20,007 shares. Each of six members of his family held one share as his nominee; he held the rest. He sold his existing business to the company in return for the shares and debentures issued to him for £10,000, thereby making him a secured creditor for that sum. The company quickly went into liquidation and its unsecured creditors, whose claims could not be met in full, tried to press their claims against Salomon himself on the basis that the company was his *alter ego* or agent. Those claims failed. The requirements of the legislation for setting up the company had been complied with and it was immaterial that Salomon held all the shares beneficially. The company had been established as a separate entity and it was that, not Salomon, with which the creditors had contracted.

Similarly, creditors of the International Tin Council could not enforce its debts against the individual states which were its members (*Rayner v DTI* (1989)). And directors will generally not incur personal liability for acts done in their capacity as such (see below, pp.56–57).

Advantages

By incorporation, therefore, a "veil" may be said to be drawn between persons dealing with a company and its members, so that direct proceedings may not generally be taken against the members themselves. Just as a third party cannot proceed against the members by ignoring the company, he may be similarly unable to proceed against the company through the medium of one of its members. In *B. v B.* (1978), a wife was unable to obtain discovery of company documents by asking the court to order her husband, who had a right as a director to inspect them, to produce them.

Disadvantages

The corporate personality rule may operate to the disadvantage of the members. Thus, in *Tunstall v Steigmann* (1962), a landlord could not resist her tenant's application for a new tenancy on the basis that she intended to carry on a business on the premises, because the business was to be carried on by a company which, though controlled by her, was nevertheless legally a separate person. Similarly under English law, a member cannot insure the company's property against destruction—it is not his property (*Macaura v Northern Assurance* (1925)); but he may have an insurable interest in the venture in which the company is engaged (*Wilson v Jones* (1867)). In *Macaura's* case, the plaintiff sold all of the timber on his estate to a company in consideration for shares in that company, of which he was also an unsecured creditor. He could not recover under policies he effected for insuring his interest against the total destruction by fire which occurred, because he personally had no insurable interest in the timber after its sale. In *Wilson v Jones*, a shareholder in the Atlantic Telegraph Company took out a marine insurance policy on the "adventure" of laying a cable from Ireland to Newfoundland, an attempt which was unsuccessful. It was held that the subject-matter of the insurance was not the company's property but the profits which he himself expected to derive from the adventure. They were lost, so he could recover. However, in Canada, the Supreme Court has allowed a person who formerly traded as an individual, and who then formed a company of which he was the sole shareholder and director, to enforce an insurance contract taken out in his own name for damage by fire to company assets (*Constitution Ins. Co. of Canada v Kosmopoulos* (1987)) and in *The Moonacre* (1992) the unsecured creditor in *Macaura* was distinguished from a person "whose" yacht was owned by a company which granted him powers of attorney which were held to confer an insurable interest upon him.

Practical Considerations

Generally, if individuals decide to become members of a limited liability company, they must accept the adverse as well as the beneficial consequences of incorporation. They benefit from being able to trade with their liability limited to the value of their shares and they may be able to obtain tax advantages from investing in this form of business association. For persons who merely wish to invest in, rather than to participate in the running of, a business enterprise, it is convenient to put their money into a company, the day-to-day activities of which can be carried on by an appointed board of directors.

As an independent entity, the company can conduct litigation on its own behalf, as claimant or defendant, and may buy, hold or sell property without reference to the individual members. In particular, it can do these things perpetually for, unlike its members, it does not have to die (although it may be wound up). By offering these advantages, the law induces investment and encourages trade.

Majority Rule

But at a price. The shareholder, depending on the size of his shareholding, is generally able to participate to some extent in company decisions by voting at meetings but he must bow to the will of the majority if that goes against him (see also the rule in *Foss v Harbottle*, below, p.89). His rights depend in part on articles of association which may be altered. His rights may be varied or he may even be paid off. Yet he cannot himself decide to leave the company and to recover the capital he invested, except insofar as he is free to sell his shares to another, who takes his place.

If a minority shareholder, he receives protection in a number of forms, e.g. as a consequence of the publicity requirements in the companies legislation, but that may also be seen as an intrusion into otherwise private affairs. Similarly, the rights of members may be protected in liquidations, but the whole procedure of winding-up is an arduous and expensive way of terminating the company.

LIFTING THE VEIL

Although the decision in the *Salomon* case remains good law, there is a large number of situations in which the veil of corporate personality may be said to be lifted, so as to expose the identity of the company's members or officers. On one hand, it may be said that the number of exceptions has become so numerous that *Salomon* has been reduced to a shadow. On the other, it is possible to find some consistency between those "exceptions" and *Salomon*.

Companies Legislation

The companies legislation contains numerous examples where *Salomon* is ignored. Thus, persons guilty of fraudulent trading may incur unlimited personal liability for the company's debts (**IA 1986 s.213**) and directors wrongfully trading during impending insolvency may be required to contribute to the company's assets on insolvency (**IA 1986 s.214**). These cases may be seen as exceptions to *Salomon* or as cases where the parties have not fulfilled conditions upon which the privilege of limited liability is granted.

Other Legislation

The courts may be faced with an unintended apparent conflict between *Salomon*, as a consequence of the Companies Acts, and the provisions of another Act of Parliament. Thus, compulsory purchase legislation normally entitles a person whose property is acquired or who is dispossessed to compensation.

KEY CASE

DHN v Tower Hamlets (1976)

DHN carried on a business on land owned by a subsidiary company, Bronze. The land was compulsorily acquired and compensation paid to Bronze. Compensation for disturbance was also payable to someone with an interest in the land. But no business of Bronze was disturbed and DHN appeared to have no interest in the land. The Court of Appeal held DHN to be entitled to compensation on the basis of the common factors in the identity of the group of companies. Otherwise, because of the companies' separate legal personalities, compensation would not have been payable in a case in which it clearly should have been.

A similar result was reached in *Smith, Stone & Knight v Birmingham* (1939) by declaring a subsidiary carrying on business on property of a holding company to be the latter's agent, thereby entitling it to compensation. *DHN* was, however, disapproved in the (distinguishable) Scottish case of *Woolfson v Strathclyde* (1978) HL.

It may be that a strict application of *Salomon* may result in giving effect to Parliament's intention in another statute. In *Lee v Lee's Air Farming* (1961), a widow received compensation for the death of her husband as an employee of the company, albeit that he was sole governing director and held 2,000 of the 3,000 shares, because it followed from *Salomon* that he could function as an officer of his company and as an employee. Whether a director can be an employee for the purposes of a particular statute is a question of fact

(*Secretary of State v Bottrill* (1999): managing director and sole shareholder could recover redundancy payment).

Apart from unintentionally enacting a statutory provision inconsistent with *Salomon*, there is, of course, no reason why the legislature cannot exercise its sovereign power directly to override *Salomon*, e.g. to fix tax liability on shareholders or directors.

A statute may give the courts discretion as to whether the corporate veil may be pierced. Hence, where an application is made to wind up a company on the "just and equitable" ground, the court may subject the exercise of the members' legal rights to equitable considerations, such as that the company is a small company formed or continued on the basis of a personal relationship involving mutual trust and confidence (*Ebrahimi v Westbourne Galleries* (1973)).

Judicial Intervention
Quite apart from such a case, the courts have not infrequently, although not as a general practice (*Adams v Cape* (1989)), taken it upon themselves to lift the veil. Their aim is usually seen to be the avoidance of clear injustice, although it is not obvious where the line may be drawn between apparent injustice which permits lifting of the veil (e.g. because the corporate edifice is a "sham" or "façade" concealing the true facts (e.g. *Kensington International v Republic of the Congo* (2005)) and that which does not. (Is it arguable in any, or all, of the following situations that they are cases to which *Salomon* should not apply anyway? *Cf. George Fischer v Multi Construction* (1994): the plaintiff holding company could recover substantial damages for loss caused to its subsidiary company by the defendant's breach of a contract with the plaintiff.)

Procedural Irregularity
Corporate decisions are generally ineffective if the correct procedure is not followed. However, if the only result of insisting on the correct procedure's being pursued is counterproductive, it may be waived. In *Re Bailey Hay* (1971), a resolution by a minority (two) of the corporators was valid although the meeting was held at too short notice, because all five corporators attended and those not voting acquiesced in the resolution.

Public Policy
Certainly, considerations of public policy are likely to override particular legal rules. Also, injustice may clearly result from improper conduct and the courts are particularly unwilling to permit the use of the corporate form in order to further improper conduct. They may go farther. In *Gilford v Horne* (1933), not only did the court grant an injunction against a former employee who had

covenanted with his employers not to solicit their customers after he left their employment; it also granted an injunction against the company he set up (albeit he was not a member) in order to carry on a business inconsistent with the covenant. In *Creasey v Breachwood* (1992), an employee wrongfully dismissed by company "A" (which was dissolved) was held entitled to proceed against company "B" (to which A's assets had been transferred without regard to the separate identity of A or the interests of its creditors). A freezing (*Mareva*) injunction can be made to restrain the disposal of interests in an interlocking network of English and foreign companies and trusts used by the defendant to conceal and safeguard his assets (*Re A Company* (1985)) and the court may decline to vary such an injunction to allow a company to pay its solicitors when they could be paid by its holding company (*Atlas v Avalon (The Coral Rose)* (1991)). Similarly, a director cannot avoid the statutory provision prohibiting loans to directors by getting the company to lend money to a puppet company of his (*Wallersteiner v Moir* (1974)).

Wrongdoing
The same approach may be used to avoid liability in "quasi-criminal" cases. A club which was an incorporated company was treated as an unincorporated association of individuals in *Trebanog Working Men's Club v Macdonald* (1904) so that its sales of liquor were matters of internal accounting, between the members, whose property the liquor was deemed to be, rather than a criminal retail sale without a licence.

KEY CASE

RE H (1996)
Where the defendant used the corporate structure of family companies as a device to conceal the fraudulent evasion of excise duty, and no useful purpose was served in involving the company in criminal proceedings, the court treated the company's property as realisable property of the shareholders in making an order under the Criminal Justice Act 1988 s.77 to restrain the defendants from dealing in their realisable property and to appoint a receiver to take possession of and manage the property.

Trust and Agency
The courts have also avoided the effects of *Salomon* by use of the concepts of trust and agency. In *The Abbey, Malvern Wells v MLGP* (1951), the company's property was impressed with the terms of a trust where the shareholders and directors were trustees under a trust deed; in effect, the company was an incorporated charitable trust.

Salomon decided that a company is not generally the agent of its members. But the courts may be willing to admit an agency relationship between companies in the same group. In *Smith, Stone & Knight v Birmingham* (1939), Atkinson J. enumerated the following tests, in deciding that a subsidiary company was the agent of its holding company:

(a) whether the profits were treated as profits of the parent company;
(b) whether the persons conducting the business were appointed by the parent company;
(c) whether the parent company was the head and brain of the business;
(d) whether the parent company governed the adventure;
(e) whether profits were made by the parent company's skill and direction; and
(f) whether the parent company was in effectual and constant control.

However, in practice it is unlikely that members will be held to have consented that a company act as their agent (*Yukong v Rendsburg* (1997)).

GROUPS

Just as individual human beings may combine for purposes of trade, so may different companies. But does it necessarily follow that, because the law *prima facie* recognises an incorporated company as an independent legal person, then it must concede completely independent character to each member of a group of companies? What effect would treating the shareholders as a whole for some purposes have on the shareholders of each company, whether they be human or corporate? The reality of group structure, whether it arises historically or by decision (e.g. for convenience or tax advantage), finds expression in the definition of a subsidiary of a holding company as: a company in which the holding company either holds a majority of the voting rights, or is a member which either controls the composition of its board of directors or, alone or by agreement with other members, controls a majority of the voting rights; or a subsidiary of another subsidiary of the holding company (**CA 2006 s.1159**). But a Panamanian company could not qualify as a German subsidiary if its shares were wholly owned by only a German individual (*The Tiburon* (1990)).

From the definition it can be ascertained, e.g. whether group accounts, as well as separate accounts of each company, must be prepared, so as to provide a true and fair view of the state of affairs and profit or loss of the group as a whole (see Chapter 17). In *Wallersteiner v Moir* (1974), a complicated arrangement of companies, trusts and so on, controlled by one man for his own purposes, was treated as a whole to see whether financial provision had been provided by a company for purchase of its own shares in contravention of the current prohibition (see pp.15–17). And in *Re BCCI (No.10)* (1994), the court approved a compromise pooling the assets of several interrelated companies, and to avoid difficult, lengthy and expensive litigation.

In *Holdsworth v Caddies* (1955), the managing director of a holding company could not claim damages for breach of contract when ordered to confine his activities to the business of a subsidiary. In *Levison v Farin* (1978), damages payable to a subsidiary were reduced by the amount of a tax benefit which shareholders would derive from a holding company; otherwise they would have benefited twice.

But in most cases the companies within a group are treated as separate persons. This can be advantageous. Thus, it is common for shipowners, though they may have several ships, to operate through "one ship companies".

KEY CASE

THE EVPO AGNIC (1988)

The shareholders and directors of the company owning the *Skipper I* (the defendant) were identical in the case of the company owning the *Evpo Agnic*. However, claimants "against" the *Skipper I* could not enforce their claim against the *Evpo Agnic* by using the procedure allowing an admiralty action *in rem* to be brought against a "sister ship" owned by the defendant, for the company owning the *Evpo Agnic* was a separate person.

Similarly, a holding company which has issued a letter of comfort expressing its intention to support its financially weak subsidiary has been held not liable for carrying on the business of the subsidiary with intent to defraud its creditors (*Re Augustus Barnett* (1985)). A company is generally entitled to arrange the affairs of a group so that liabilities fall on individual companies within that group: thus, liabilities of foreign subsidiaries may be unenforceable against a holding company in this jurisdiction (*Adams v Cape* (1989)).

There are likewise disadvantages. A holding company cannot normally take advantage of a contract between a subsidiary and a third party for the holding company's benefit (*The Eurymedon* (1974)). In the *Multinational Gas* case (1983), a subsidiary company could not sue its shareholders (three oil companies) or its allegedly negligent directors, for the shareholders could act in their own interests and owed no duty to the company, and the shareholders' approval of the directors' acts made them acts of the company; a second subsidiary could, however, be liable. Is the decision realistic?

Supporting Subsidiaries

Organisation of a business by means of a number of legally distinct companies can be administratively convenient for companies and enable them to reap the benefits of the profitable trading, whilst isolating them from the liabilities, of subsidiaries. However, liability may be incurred other than by a piercing of the veil. Thus, it may well be that auditors will not sign the accounts of, and third parties will be reluctant to trade with, a financially suspect subsidiary without evidence of its being supported by its holding company. One, not uncommon, way of doing this is for the parent company to provide financial assistance direct to its subsidiary—though that may be minimal reassurance to third parties if the parent remains free to withdraw such assistance at any time. A second possibility is for the parent to guarantee the obligations of its subsidiary, though naturally no person, corporate or otherwise, will commit himself to direct liability under a guarantee if he can avoid it.

A practice has developed, therefore, of holding companies issuing statements of assurance in relation to the activities and stability of subsidiaries. It is clearly in the interests of the issuers of such documents that they should fall short of committing them to contractual liability to parties dealing with the company in question, so they should be drafted to demonstrate the absence of intention to contract. This will be a matter of construction.

KEY CASE

KLEINWORT BENSON V MALAYSIA MINING CORP. (1987)

In order that the plaintiff bank would lend money to its subsidiary, the defendant holding company supplied the bank with a "letter of comfort" stating that it was its policy to ensure that the subsidiary was at all times in a position to meet its liabilities to the bank. The subsidiary collapsed and the defendant withdrew support from it but was held not liable to the bank for damages for its loss in being unable to recover the loan from the subsidiary. The letter was merely a present statement of fact as to the defendant's intentions, not a contractual promise as to its future conduct.

If there is no liability in contract in such a case and the parent company has fraudulently induced the third party to deal with the subsidiary to its detriment, the third party may recover damages for deceit from the parent. There is also the possibility of liability under **IA 1986 s.213** (below, p.107) for fraudulent trading (*cf. Re Augustus Barnett*, above, p.45).

CHARACTER OF THE CORPORATE PERSON

Despite the separation of the company from its members, it may be necessary to look at the members in order to ascertain some details about the company itself. In *Daimler v Continental Tyre* (1916), a company incorporated in England with a British subject (who had one share) as its Secretary could not sue in the English courts in wartime because the controllers (all the directors and the other shareholders) were enemy aliens, resident in Germany. Thus, residence, domicile or nationality may be gleaned from the identity of the members. However, companies, unlike natural persons, are creatures of national law. Thus, although the EU Treaty permits freedom of establishment by natural and corporate persons of one Member State in another (e.g. by setting up subsidiaries), companies incorporated in a particular Member State do not have any inherent right to transfer their central management, control and administration to another Member State while retaining their status as a company incorporated under the law of the first Member State (*R. v H.M. Treasury Ex p. Daily Mail* (1988)).

Companies are formed to carry on business. They may act through servants or agents but the acts of one of a company's organs (see Chapter 13) may be identified with acts of the company itself. Thus, the acts of a managing director, as the company's "directing mind and will", have been attributed to the company (*Lennard's Carrying v Asiatic Petroleum*, 1915). Where a fraud was perpetrated by a company whose directing mind and will was its sole shareholder, the fraud was attributed to the company itself, which was therefore unable to claim against its auditors for failing to detect it (*Stone & Rolls v Moore Stephens* (2009) HL).

However, the basic question is who, for the purposes of the issue under consideration, controls the relevant company activity (*Meridian v Securities Commission* (1995): company liable where investment managers failed to discharge statutory duty to disclose substantial holdings).

Hence, the corporate person is able to form an intention (*Bolton v Graham* (1956)). And a company may be liable for knowing receipt of stolen funds knowingly received by its chairman of the board (*El Ajou v Dollar* (1993)). In *Burmah Oil v Bank of England* (1981), a company was held not to be able to set aside a contract allegedly entered under economic duress because, although ruin was staring the company in the face, it was not so staring any of the board members personally, who could therefore still act dispassionately.

A director answering interrogatories served on a company must act reasonably to inquire of all officers, servants and agents who might reasonably be contacted and have the relevant knowledge, therefore known to the company—not just the directors (*Stanfield Properties v National Westminster Bank* (1983)).

It does not follow that, because a company is capable of action and has legal personality, it must be equated with natural persons (not all of whom have the same legal capacity anyway). Thus, whereas a company may enter into a partnership with an entertainer to do things which only a natural person can do (*Newstead v Frost* (1978)), it was held unable to worship so as to enable it to breach the **Sunday Observance Act 1677** (*Rolloswin v Chromolit* (1970)). And, in the view of Lord Denning M.R. in *B.S.C. v Granada* (1981), the privilege against self-discrimination is not available to a corporation. "It has no body to be kicked or soul to be damned." Nonetheless, a company has human rights, such as to privacy, though they may not be the same as individuals' human rights (*R. v Broadcasting Standards Commission Ex p. BBC* (2000)).

Capacity

9

THE *ULTRA VIRES* DOCTRINE

It was formerly necessary for a company's memorandum of association to indicate the objects which it is intended the company should pursue; and traditionally it also included a statement of the powers expressly conferred upon it to enable it to achieve those objects. Until recently, the memorandum was taken to state the prima facie extent of its powers, so that anything else done by the company was ultra vires, outside its powers, and something it was legally incapable of doing.

The reasons for the ultra vires doctrine were basically two-fold. Shareholders who invested money in a company were considered to be entitled to see that it was applied for the purposes for which they were presumably induced to invest and not to see it dissipated in uncontemplated ventures. And those who advanced credit to a company were entitled to rely on its creditworthiness so far as that could be ascertained from, inter alia, its statement of objects and powers.

However, the strength of the doctrine was eroded by the ingenuity of draftsmen of memoranda of association (with the compliance of the courts), the power to alter the memorandum and the enactment in 1972 of **art.9(1)** of the first **EEC Directive on Company Law (1968)** (now codified as **Directive 2009/101 EC**) that: "Acts done by the organs of the company shall be binding upon it, even if those acts are not within the objects of the company, unless such acts exceed the powers that the law confers or allows to be conferred on those organs."

The ultra vires doctrine became less of a protection for members and creditors and more of an obstacle that might have arisen unexpectedly to invalidate an apparently intra vires transaction. It has therefore formally been abolished.

OBJECTS AND POWERS

Provisions in the memorandum existing before the enactment of the **CA 2006** are now treated as part of the company's articles of association (**CA 2006 s.28**), so many companies will automatically have statements of objects and powers unless they remove them; and it remains permissible for a company to state its intended objects and powers if it chooses to do so. However, this is no longer necessary; and the validity of an act done by a company cannot be called into question by any person (whether the company or the person with whom it is dealing) on the ground of lack of capacity by reason of anything in the company's memorandum (**CA 2006 s.39**).

However, though a transaction will not be invalid because of the company's constitution, it may be invalid for other reasons (e.g. directors' conflict of interests: *Co-operative Rabobank v Minderhoud* (1998) ECJ). Similarly, the mere fact that a company has capacity to do something does not mean that an act purportedly done on its behalf is legally binding; the person acting must have authority to bind the company. It is, therefore, further provided that, in favour of a person dealing with a company in good faith, the power of the board of directors to bind the company, or authorise others to do so, is deemed to be free of any limitation under the company's constitution (**CA 2006 s.40(1)**; *Ford v Polymer Vision* (2009)). However, the power of any other body or person (e.g. a single director) to confer authority on a would-be agent of the company may be subject to limitations.

A person dealing with a company is not bound to enquire as to any limitations on the powers of the directors to bind the company or authorize others to do so; and he is presumed to have acted in good faith unless the contrary is proved; in particular, he is not to be regarded as acting in bad faith by reason only of his knowing that an act is beyond the powers of the directors under the company's constitution (**CA 2006 s.40**). **Section 40** may even avail a director, as incidentally "a person dealing with the company"— but not if the director is the chairman, whose duty is to uphold its constitution (*Smith v Henniker-Major* (2002)); and it does not avail a shareholder receiving bonus shares (*EIC Services v Phipps* (2004) CA). It has been suggested that an absence of bad faith under the statute will not necessarily relieve the third party of liability in equity as a constructive trustee (*cf. International Sales v Marcus* (1981)), although it may equally be said that such a view introduces an unwarranted limitation on the provision.

The protection generally afforded to third parties dealing with the company is restricted by **CA 2006 s.41**, where the relevant "third party" is not sufficiently independent of the company. Where a company enters into a transaction to which the parties include a director of the company or its holding company or a person connected with such a director, the transaction is voidable at the instance of the company *vis-à-vis* such a person. Such persons (unless they are not directors and did not know the directors were exceeding their powers) and directors who authorise such transactions are liable to account for gains made, and to indemnify for losses resulting from, the transaction. The transaction ceases to be voidable if:

(a) restitution of the subject-matter of the transaction is no longer possible, or

(b) the company is indemnified for any loss resulting from the transaction, or

(c) rights acquired *bona fide* for value and without actual notice of the directors' excess of powers by someone not party to the transaction would be affected, or

(d) the transaction is ratified by the company in general meeting, by any necessary ordinary or special resolution.

Where such transactions are valid in favour of independent persons, such a person or company may, however, apply to the court for an order affirming, severing or setting aside the transaction on such terms as appear to the court to be just.

Whatever the position as between the company and outsiders, except in the case of an act to be done in fulfilment of a legal obligation arising from an act already done by the company, a member of the company has a right to bring proceedings to restrain the doing of any act which falls outside the powers of the directors (**CA 2006 s.40(4)**). Indeed, the validation of acts between the company and outsiders does not affect any liability incurred by the directors, or any other person, by reason of the directors' exceeding their powers (**CA 2006 s.40(5)**).

However, it is the duty of the directors to act within their powers (**CA 2006 s.171**: see below, p.76).

Liability for Officers and Agents; Contracts

The liability of a company for crimes and torts will be discussed in Chapter 11. However, it may briefly be noted here that a company's liability for tortious acts usually depends on an application of the test of course of employment under the ordinary tort rules of vicarious liability rather than on issues of company law. And its criminal liability may be narrow, given the usual necessity for mens rea and the restricted scope of vicarious liability in criminal law, unless the "directing mind" is that of the actor.

A contract may (subject to ordinary rules on contract formalities) be made by a company itself, by writing under its common seal, or on behalf of a company, by any person acting under its authority, express or implied (**CA 2006 s.43**). The company's liability for contracts depends on, first, the effect of the rules on capacity and, secondly, the authority of the person(s) contracting for the company. As seen in Chapter 9, the effect of **CA 1985 ss.39–40** means that an attack on a transaction should not fail on the ground that the company is without capacity to act or that the board of directors is incapable of authorising an agent to act on behalf of the company. It nonetheless remains to be considered exactly when an agent has authority to bind the company.

A contract made by the company itself (through one of its organs) will obviously bind it. But what of a contract made on behalf of the company by a person acting as an agent?

An agent who has been expressly authorised to act can bind the company with respect to matters within his express, implied or usual authority. An "agent" with no authority at all will not bind the company unless the company later ratifies his acts (*ING v R&V* (2006)), which it will wish to do if it wants to enforce the contract. Otherwise, the party attempting to contract with the company (the "contractor") may be able to sue the agent for breach of warranty of authority (*Firbank's Executors v Humphreys* (1886)).

An agent with no authority as described above (because he exceeds his authority or because he has been given none) or whose acts are not ratified may bind the company if he acts within his apparent or ostensible authority. He may have to indemnify the company for making it liable but the contractor can sue the company directly.

OSTENSIBLE AUTHORITY

In *Freeman & Lockyer v Buckhurst Park Properties (Mangal)* (1964), a company was bound by a contract entered into by a person acting as its managing director with its consent, although he had not been formally appointed. There are four conditions for such liability.

1 A representation must be made to the contractor that the agent had authority to enter on behalf of the company into a contract of the kind sought to be enforced.

The directors are the company's usual agents. Furthermore, the acts of a person acting as a director are valid notwithstanding a defect in his appointment, disqualification from holding office, his ceasing to hold office or his not being entitled to vote on the matter in issue (**CA 2006 s.161**). Even so, the directors must normally exercise their powers as a board; and an individual director or other person will only be able to exercise the board's powers by delegation or by a representation by the board that the individual has authority. Such authority may usually be delegated to the managing director.

> ### KEY CASE
>
> **PANORAMA V FIDELIS (1971)**
> A company was bound to pay for cars hired by the company secretary, ostensibly for carrying the company's customers. The modern company secretary, being more than a mere clerk, has extensive duties and responsibilities and has authority to enter contracts for administrative purposes, without necessarily having authority relating to the commercial management of the company.

2 The representation must be made by a person or persons having "actual" authority to manage the business of the company either generally or in respect of those matters to which the contract relates.

Thus, a director without authority cannot, simply by saying that he has it, give himself ostensible authority (see *Armagas v Mundogas (The Ocean Frost)* (1986), below, p.58). But, if the board acquiesces in his exercise of such authority, the company may be bound (*Hely-Hutchinson v Brayhead* (1967)). And, if a company confers actual or ostensible authority to enter a specific transaction, a representation by the agent as to his authority (e.g. that his sole signature suffices) is capable of being relied on as an act of holding out (*Ebeed v Soplex* (1984). (*Cf. ING v R&V* (2006), holding that an agent with apparent authority may authorise another agent; and *First Energy v H.I.B.* (1993), holding that an unauthorised agent may have ostensible authority to communicate whether he has become authorised!—distinguished in *Hudson Bay Apparel v Umbro* (2010) CA, following *The Ocean Frost*). Similarly, a forged document apparently sealed or signed on behalf of the company will not bind it (*Ruben v Great Fingall* (1906)) unless someone with authority represents it as the company's. A purchaser can rely on a document executed by two authorised signatories or by a director in the presence of a witness (**Law of Property Act 1925 s.74(1); CA 2006 s.44**).

3 The contractor must, by relying on the representation, be induced thereby to enter into the contract.

A contractor might argue that, since he has constructive notice of the company's public documents, he can therefore rely on a representation of authority contained therein (such as that the board may delegate certain authority to an individual director). This is wrong. He will only be able to rely on a provision therein if he has actual knowledge of it; otherwise there is no reliance (*Rama v Proved Tin* (1952)).

4 There must be no circumstance precluding the contractor's reliance.

(a) It was formerly the rule that the company's public documents should not demonstrate a lack of authority to enter the relevant contract or to delegate authority to an agent to enter it and, as the contractor had constructive notice of the public documents, then, he was bound by limitations therein. (Thus, he was deemed to know of lack of authority where it could only be given by a resolution which had to be filed, and none had been.) **CA 1985 s.711A(1)** abolished that rule, the exceptions to it remaining effective:

(i) In *Royal British Bank v Turquand* (1856), the board of directors could borrow money on bond if authorised by a resolution. The lending bank could enforce such a transaction although no resolution had been passed. "Finding that the authority might be made complete by a resolution, [the contractor] would have a right to infer the fact of a resolution authorising that which on the face of the document appeared to be legitimately done." A contractor is entitled to assume that acts of "internal management" (which do not have to be made public) have been carried out. The *Turquand* defence only applies if expressly pleaded (*Rolled Steel v BSC* (1984)).

(ii) Certain defects are expressly covered (e.g. **CA 2006 s.161**, above, p.53). Subject to contrary proof, minuted meetings of members or directors are deemed duly held and appointments of directors and managers deemed valid (**CA 2006 s.249(2)(c)**). But the contractor will not be assisted by the curing of defects if there has been no appointment at all (*Morris v Kanssen* (1946)).

(iii) A contractor may generally enforce a contract authorised by the board of directors despite restrictions on capacity or authority of which he is unaware (**CA 2006 ss.39–41**: Chapter 9, above).

(b) The contractor must not have actual knowledge of the lack of authority (*Rolled Steel v BSC* (1984)).

(c) The circumstances must not be such that he should be put on inquiry (*Hopkins v Dallas* (2004)). Where **CA 2006 s.40** applies (above pp.50) a contractor must act in good faith; but this is presumed, unless proved otherwise, and he is not bound to enquire into lack of capacity or authority.

Crimes and Torts

11

CRIMES

Different crimes may provide different bases for a company or one of its officers or employees to be liable or able to plead a defence. An officer or employee may be personally liable. Thus, as legislation commonly does, the Trade Descriptions Act 1968 made express provision for the liability of any director, manager, secretary or similar officer where an offence committed by a body corporate had been with his consent or connivance (see *Tesco v Nattrass* (1971)). The liability of an employee may make the company vicariously liable, though of course the company may have a defence. In *Tesco v Brent LBC* (1993) Tesco could not avail itself of the defence of ignorance that a video purchaser was under age, since the knowledge of the selling employee was the knowledge of the company for the purposes of the relevant legislation; but in *Tesco v Nattrass* it was not liable for an assistant's display of articles in contravention of the **Trade Descriptions Act 1968**, otherwise the statutory defence that the act was committed due to the act or default of another person would have been illusory.

Criminal liability is more likely to be incurred by the company directly rather that vicariously, if the person actually committing the crime can be identified with the company as its "directing mind and will" or controller (*Att-Gen's Reference (No.2) of 1999* (2000); see above, p.47) or the intention is to impose liability for acts of someone senior in the company (e.g. *Seaboard v Secretary of State* (1994)). Indeed, a company may incur liability for the chairman's criminal intention to steal property innocently acquired by an employee for the owner (*Deutsche Genossenschaftsbank v Burnhope* (1995)); and Parliament may provide that a corporate employer cannot avoid strict liability for reasonably practicable steps to ensure health and safety just because senior management or the "directing mind" had taken reasonable care (*R. v British Steel* (1994)).

Companies have thereby been held guilty of intent to deceive (*D.P.P. v Kent Contractors* (1944); *Moore v Bresler* (1944)). Under the **Corporate Manslaughter and Corporate Homicide Act 2007**, a corporation is guilty of an offence if the way in which its activities are managed or organised causes a person's death and amounts to a gross breach of a duty of care as specified in the Act.

Since the legal personality of the company is distinct from that of its members or officers, it can be guilty of conspiracy with them or others (*R. v I.C.R. Haulage* (1944)—conspiracy to defraud). But it takes two to make a conspiracy and the crime cannot be committed by the company and its sole director (*R. v McDonnell* (1966)). Furthermore, the Court of Appeal has recoiled from finding a conspiracy between the directors and a company which was the victim of the alleged conspiracy (*Belmont v Williams* (1978)). Where shareholders or directors act illegally or dishonestly in relation to a company, knowledge of the dishonesty is not to be imputed to the company (*Att-Gen's Reference (No.2 of 1983)*: directors guilty of theft of money controlled and *de facto* owned by them).

A company will not automatically be liable for all the criminal activities of its servants or agents. The contrary policy of the relevant legislation may be revealed as a matter of statutory interpretation. In *Tesco v Nattrass* (1971), Tesco was held not liable for an assistant's display of articles for sale in contravention of the Trade Descriptions Act 1968. To hold the company liable would make illusory the statutory defence that the offence was committed due to the act or default of another person. Moreover, the Act made express provision for the liability of any director, manager, secretary or similar officer where an offence committed by a body corporate had been committed with his consent or connivance.

Liability falling on a "manager" will not extend beyond those in positions of real authority (*R. v Boal* (1992)).

. . . .

TORTS

A company will be tortiously liable for the act of a natural person if it constitutes an act of the company or the company is vicariously liable for it (e.g. *New Zealand Guardian Trust v Brooks* (1994)). The company may be liable though the employee's act was forbidden (*Re Supply of Ready Mixed Concrete* (1994)).

Traditionally, if an individual commits a tort for which the company is liable, both he and the company will be liable. However, maintaining the effectiveness of limited liability (albeit that it is designed to protect shareholders), where liability arises from an assumption of liability, directors will not normally be personally liable for acts in their capacity as directors (e.g. negligent preparation of advice given by company) without specific assumption of liability (*Williams v Natural Life* (1998); *cf. Standard Chartered Bank v Pakistan National Shipping Corp* (2002): director liable for fraud). The company and the director may be jointly liable where the director does more than carry out his constitutional role as a director (*MCA Records v Charly* (2001)).

A servant would not usually have the necessary authority to commit a tort during an unauthorised activity (*Poulton v LSWR* (1867)). But the company will be vicariously liable for a servant's or agent's tort committed during an otherwise authorised activity if he has acted within the scope of his employment (because he is expressly or impliedly authorised or the act is incidental to his course of employment). The policies of the law of tort in imposing vicarious liability may be said to justify the liability of a company which actually authorises its employee's tort (*Campbell v Paddington* (1911)).

A company can be held liable for damages where the company holds out an employee as acting within the course of his employment and a third party suffers loss by reliance on that representation. But the company will not be liable where the representation is not made by those empowered to perform acts of the company.

KEY CASE

ARMAGAS V MUNDOGAS (THE OCEAN FROST) (1986)

The defendant company's chartering manager (a vice-president) purported to enter on behalf of the defendants into a three-year charter-party with the plaintiff shipowners, representing that he had the authority to do so, albeit he was in fact only entitled to do so for one year. The defendants were not vicariously liable for his deceit because the misrepresentation was made not by them nor by someone authorised to act on their behalf but by the employee himself. The mere fact that a person is employed does not render his employer liable for everything done during his employment or automatically give him power to bind his employer by representing his authority to be greater than it is in fact.

Rights of Members

12

EFFECT OF THE COMPANY'S CONSTITUTION

What are the rights of a shareholder arising from his agreement to become a member and by what methods may his rights be altered?

The relationship between a member of a company and the company itself is determined by the terms of: the memorandum of association (the significance of which is considerably less than formerly: see above, Chapter 9); the articles of association; and any resolutions or agreements made by the company (specifically those to which **CA 2006 ss.29–30** apply). The Act refers to the articles and such resolutions and agreements as its constitution (**CA 2006 s.17**).

The provisions of a company's constitution bind the company and its members as if they were covenants on the part of the company and each member to observe its provisions (**CA 2006 s.33**). Thus, a member can enforce a provision enabling him to require the directors to purchase shares he wished to transfer (*Rayfield v Hands* (1959)) and a company can enforce a provision requiring resort to arbitration before judicial proceedings can be taken (*Hickman v Kent Sheepbreeders* (1915)). Shareholders are entitled to be treated equally according to their rights and obligations under **CA 2006 s.33** (e.g. so that calls are not made on certain shareholders alone) but there is no further implied obligation that they are not to be discriminated against by the board of directors or the general meeting (e.g. if further shares are not allotted to members in a jurisdiction with onerous disclosure requirements: *Mutual Life v Rank* (1981)).

The agreement between each of the members and the company has commonly been termed a contract. Accordingly, they should be construed according to principles of contractual interpretation, in a business like way. Thus, clear terms must be given effect, unless this would be commercially absurd (*Thompson v Goblin Hill Hotels* (2011) PC (Jamaica)); but an express term to appoint a director by a group of shareholders with a certain percentage of shares may be subject to an implied term that the appointment should cease when the shareholding falls below the threshold (*A-G of Belize v Belize Telecom* (2009) PC (Belize)). Nonetheless, this subject to the general rules of company law. The Act does not term it a contract and, if it is one, it is a contract of a special kind. Hence, although certain contractual remedies are available (declaration; injunction; action for a liquidated sum, e.g. dividends), some are not (rectification of the articles: *Scott v Scott* (1940)). The courts have been reluctant to grant damages for fear of reducing capital (see Chapter 4) or enabling the member to recover more than the dividends due if the regulations in the articles were observed.

It has been suggested that each member has a right to have the company's affairs conducted in accordance with the articles. This may seem somewhat contrary to the principles of majority rule (Chapter 16) but even those principles admit exceptions and the view propounded makes eminent sense in the case of small companies which are akin to partnerships. Furthermore, despite the general abolition of the ultra *vires* doctrine, a member has a right to bring proceedings to restrain the doing of an act which falls outside the powers of the directors (**CA 2006 s.40(4)**).

Only the members as such can take advantage of the provisions in the articles. Third parties do not acquire rights under the **Contracts (Rights of Third Parties) Act 1999 (s.6(2))**. Thus, a director sued by the company qua director cannot enforce an article stipulating for arbitration, even if he is also a member (*Beattie v Beattie* (1938)). And a non-member cannot enforce an article which stipulates that he should be the company solicitor (*Eley v Positive Government* (1876)). There is nothing to prevent a contract being made between the company and the third party on terms incorporating the articles of association but, since the articles may by statute be varied, that contract is variable. So, for example, a contract of employment might be terminated without compensation (*Read v Astoria* (1952)). Even a contract on fixed terms cannot oust the statutory power to alter the articles but such an alteration, although effective, may constitute a breach of contract with the non-member entitling him to compensation (*Shindler v Northern Raincoat* (1960)).

ALTERATION OF THE ARTICLES

CA 2006 s.21 provides that, if it is for its benefit (*Citco v Pusser's* (2007) PC), a company may by special resolution alter its articles, as may all the corporators acting together, independently of the section (*Cane v Jones* (1979)). The articles as altered remain subject to alteration. The court may order alteration of the articles for unfair prejudice; if the order prohibits a further alteration without the court's leave, the company has no power to make a further inconsistent alteration without such leave (**CA 2006 s.996**).

Although the company is entitled to exercise fully the rights it already has (e.g. to impose a lien on a member's shares: *Allen v Gold Reefs* (1900)), it cannot alter the articles so as to increase the liability of a member, e.g. by requiring him to subscribe for more shares or by increasing his liability to contribute to the company's share capital without written agreement (**CA 2006 s.25**) or to do anything that a general meeting cannot do (*Secretary of State v Doffman (No.2)* (2010)).

VARIATION OF CLASS RIGHTS

Where there is more than one type of share in a company, the holders of a different species of share are said to belong to different classes of shareholders. If there is only one class of share, the articles may be altered to enable the creation of another class (*Andrews v Gas Meter*, 1897). The articles may deem a reduction of capital to be a variation of class rights (*Re Northern Engineering* (1994)).

Rights in the articles may be:
(a) rights attached to a class of shares (e.g. voting rights);
(b) rights conferred on a member in an individual capacity;
(c) "class rights," i.e. rights conferred on the beneficiary as a member of the company but not attached to any particular class of shares (*Cumbrian Newspapers v Cumberland Herald* (1986)).

CA 2006 ss.630–635 governs variation or abrogation of class rights. Class rights contained in articles with no variation of rights clause may be varied if either (a) the holders of three-quarters of the issued shares of that class consent in writing or (b) a meeting of the class sanctions the variation by special resolution. Often the articles include an express variation of rights clause, in which case the method laid down is normally compulsory.

Usually, if 15 per cent of shareholders of a company having a share capital did not consent to the variation, they may apply to the court, whose sanction is necessary for the variation to be effective (**CA 2006 s.633**). In any event, a majority is not entitled to use its power to vary class rights in fraud on the minority; a resolution may be invalid unless passed *bona fide* for the benefit of the company as a whole (see Chapter 16). This protection may, however, be insufficient in practice.

KEY CASE

GREENHALGH V ARDERNE (1951)

In *Greenhalgh v Arderne* (1951), majority shareholders, with 50,000 votes, secured a resolution converting their 10s. shares to 2s. shares, thus ensuring their ability to prevent Greenhalgh, whose shares continued to carry 20,000 votes, from blocking any resolution they supported. They could, therefore, subsequently alter the articles to enable shares to be transferred to non-members with the sanction of an ordinary resolution, thus depriving Greenhalgh of his previous right of pre-emption as a member.

A company must generally notify the Registrar of a variation of rights or the creation of a new class of shares.

Management, Receivership and Administration

13

COMPANY STRUCTURE

By incorporation, there is formed a corporate person which is separate from the servants who work for it or the shareholders who are members of it, whether it be a small family company, the shareholders of which actively participate in decision making and day-to-day administration, or a large industrial concern, wherein ownership (by the shareholders) and management (by the board of directors) may be largely divorced from each other. The organic structure of this corporate person and the constitutional relationship between the company's different organs are determined by the decisions of the members recorded in the articles of association and resolutions of meetings. In this fashion they determine how decisions are to be effected and how acts of the organs take effect as acts of the company itself.

The constitution is, like the company, set apart from the individual members and servants of the company. It may be changed but is fully effective until changed.

The primary organ is the general meeting of the shareholders. It provides the forum in which all members are prima facie entitled to participate and vote. Invariably it will devolve powers of management to another organ, the board of directors, but retaining the ultimate authority in general policy and decision-making, albeit decision-making in general meeting may be manipulated by the board. Public companies must have at least two directors and private companies at least one (**CA 2006 s.154**). The term "director" is wide enough to include for certain purposes a "shadow director", anyone in accordance with whose instructions management is carried on (**CA 2006 s.251(2)**; *Secretary of State v Deverell* (1999)).

The power of decision as to the following generally rests in the general meeting: winding-up; changes in the memorandum and articles; payment of dividends; changes in capital structure; disposal of a substantial part of the undertaking; and the appointment, remuneration and control of directors. In addition, the general meeting can generally act where the board is unwilling or unable (e.g. because of deadlock) to exercise its powers (*Barron v Potter* (1914)).

Relationship between General Meeting and Board of Directors

The relationship between the general meeting and the board is not entirely clear. In theory, the ultimate decision-making power lies in the general meeting. It can override the wishes of the directors and take away from them the powers devolved to them. In practice, it tends to follow the lead suggested by the directors, so conflict is unlikely to arise. What if it does? In principle, the matter may be resolved by construction of the articles of association. However, the question remains if the articles are unclear.

The older view is that the board is merely the agent of the general meeting, which retains the power to exercise the board's powers if it chooses to do so. In *Marshall's Valve Gear v Manning* (1909), the board decided 2:1 not to sue a person infringing the company's patent. But the general meeting (in which the dissenting director was the majority shareholder) could sue. The modern view has developed from a case distinguished in *Marshall* on the ground that the relevant articles required an extraordinary resolution to override the board, *Automatic Self-Cleansing v Cunninghame* (1906). Hence, an ordinary resolution to sell the company's undertaking was ineffective to override the board's refusal to exercise its authority to sell company property on terms it saw fit. The conclusion (now confirmed by *Breckland Group Holdings v London & Suffolk Properties* (1988)) is that, once the general meeting has devolved powers, it can only exercise them itself after first taking them back from the directors.

The relationship between the general meeting and the board of directors is important in connection with breaches of duty by the directors. If they act outside their powers, their acts can be ratified by the company if it has full knowledge of the circumstances (*Bamford v Bamford* (1969)). But it is not clear whether the board is entitled to postpone a decision on something *prima facie* within its powers in order to obtain a prior decision on the point by the general meeting in the exercise of a power previously devolved to the board. It has, however, been held that the general meeting can confer prior authority on the directors to do what is otherwise a breach of duty if the board's powers are not usurped and the notice of the meeting clearly indicates the nature of the proposed breach (*Winthrop v Winns* (1975)).

. . . .

EMPLOYEE INVOLVEMENT

Decision-making is traditionally viewed from the perspectives of the owners of the shares in the company (the "members" in general meeting) and the higher managerial officials (the directors). In recent years attention has been focused more on the company's employees. Thus, directors must have regard to the interests of employees (**CA 2006 s.172(1)(b)**); on cessation or transfer of a business, the company may make provision for employees (**CA 2006 s.247**); and the directors' annual report must include information about the company's employees (**CA 2006 s.417(5)(b)(ii)**).

There are a variety of ways in which company employees can more actively become involved with the prosperity which they help generate.

One method is to form a co-operative, borrowing capital at interest for a venture in which they participate equally in decision making and distribution of profits.

Another possibility is the establishment of a profit-sharing scheme under which shares may be allocated for the sake of employees, with the benefit of certain tax concessions. ("Employees' share scheme" is defined by **CA 2006 s.1166**.)

More widely known have been proposals for the introduction of a scheme of industrial democracy, advocated by those who may wish to curb the powers of the growing managerial class, to give effect to the idea of a company as a social or economic enterprise between capitalists and workers and/or to recognise the increased importance of plant-level collective bargaining and of consultation over confrontation. This was considered by the Bullock Committee on Industrial Democracy (1977), and "co-determination" has been implemented in some EU Member States, but it is not currently a live issue in the United Kingdom.

However, where an SE is formed and there is employee participation in the board of one of its national companies, other EU Member States wherein the SE is registered must provide for similar arrangements (**Council Directive 2001/86**, implemented in the **European Public Limited-Liability Company Regulations 2004 Pt 3**).

. . . .
CORPORATE GOVERNANCE

In 1992, the **Cadbury Committee on Corporate Governance** (i.e. the system by which companies are directed and controlled) published a **Code of Best Practice**. It recommended that all listed companies and as many other companies as possible should comply with it and publish with their annual reports and accounts details of compliance. It recommended that: the board should effectively control the company and monitor its executive management; there should be a division and balance of responsibilities and control at the head of the company, with no one individual having unfettered decision-making power, and a strong and independent element on the board; effective and largely independent non-executive directors; company secretaries should be removable only by the whole board and responsible for ensuring compliance with procedures and regulations; directors' service contracts should not exceed three years without shareholder approval; full disclosure of all directors' emoluments; effective auditing; and an obligation on directors (honestly) to report that the business is a going concern. These recommendations led, via the Greenbury Committee Report (1995) to the Hampel Committee's Combined Code on Corporate Governance and Best Practice (2003), subsequently supplemented by the Turnbull guidance for directors on the application and interpretation of the **Code (1999)**, promoting internal controls to protect shareholder interests and company assets, and the suggestions on Good Practice from the Higgs' Report (2002) on non-executive directors. The Code was revised by the Financial Reporting Council in 2006 and 2008. Its current incarnation is the UK Corporate Governance Code (2010). Listed companies are required in their annual report to declare the extent to which they have complied with the Code or to explain why and how they have not ("comply or explain").

Influenced by deliberations of the Company Law Review Steering Group, CA **2006 s.417** now provides that, unless the company is subject to the small companies' regime, the directors' annual report must contain a *business review*. It is ostensibly for the benefit of shareholders, to provide them with information to assess how the directors have performed their duty (in s.172) to promote the success of the company. However, directors must at least have regard to, and report upon, *inter alia* to employees' interests and to the environmental, social and community impact of company operations (**CA 2006 ss.172(1), 417(5)(b)**).

DIRECTORS

Qualification

Directors are appointed individually for the period specified in the articles. A private company must have at least one director and a public company at least two (**CA 2006 s.154**). A director need not be a member of the company; and another company may be a director, but a company must have at least one director who is a natural person (**CA 2006 s.155**).

Disqualification

There is no maximum age limit but a director should generally not be aged below sixteen (**CA 2006 s.157**), although minority is no excuse for acts of a director who was not entitled to act as such (**CA 2006 s.161**).

A person must not without the court's leave act as a director or be concerned in the promotion, formation or management of a company if he:

(a) is an undischarged bankrupt (**Company Directors Disqualification Act 1986 s.11**),

(b) has failed to pay under a county court administration order (**CDDA 1986 s.12**), or

(c) is the subject of a disqualification order.

Disqualification Orders and Undertakings

Under **CDDA 1986 s.1**, a court may, for a specified period (which varies but cannot exceed 15 years) order that a person:

(a) shall not be a director of a company, act as receiver of a company's property, or be involved in the promotion, formation or management of a company, without the court's leave; and

(b) shall not act as an insolvency practitioner.

Under **CDDA 1986 s.1A**, in specified circumstances the Secretary of State may accept a person's disqualification undertaking, not to do (a) or (b).

The relevant circumstances for a disqualification order are:

(a) conviction of an indictable offence in connection with (though not necessarily involving: *R. v Goodman* (1992)) the promotion, formation, management or liquidation of a company or with the receivership or management of a company's property (**CDDA 1986 s.2**) (the offence need not relate to, but must have a factual connection with, the management of a company (*R. v Goodman* (1992));

(b) persistent breaches of the companies legislation requiring any return, account or other document to be registered (**CDDA 1986 s.3**);

(c) fraud (**CDDA 1986 s.4**);

(d) a summary conviction for breaches of the companies legislation (**CDDA 1986 s.5**);

(e) conduct appearing to the Secretary of State to make him unfit to be concerned in the management of a company (**CDDA 1986 ss.8–9**) (it is no excuse that prohibited conduct is widespread and necessary to obtain business: *Re Chapman* (2003));

(f) participation in fraudulent or wrongful trading under **IA 1986 ss.213–214** (**CDDA 1986 s.10**).

Additionally

(g) the court must disqualify a director if the company commits a breach of competition law and his conduct makes him unfit to be concerned in the management of a company (**CDDA 1986 s.9A**).

Unfitness is a question of law and does not depend, for example, on a person's liability for professional negligence (*Re Barings (No.5)* (2000)) or acquittal in criminal proceedings (*Re TransTec (No.2)* 2006).

The court must (*Re Grayan* (1994)) make a disqualification order against a *de jure* or *de facto* (*Re Kaytech* (1998)) director of an insolvent company if his conduct makes him unfit to be concerned in the management of a company (**CDDA 1986 s.6**), causing the company to trade whilst insolvent and with no reasonable prospect of paying off creditors (*Secretary of State v Creegan* (2001)).

The court may make such an order against foreigners and in respect of conduct abroad (*Re Seagull (No.2)* (1993)) and, since disqualification proceedings are in the public interest, need not delay them simply because there are parallel civil proceedings concerning the same subject-matter (*Re Rex Williams Leisure* (1994)).

In exercising its discretionary power to make a disqualification order, the court will apply natural justice, in a flexible way, and take a broad view as to whether, on balance, a director's overall conduct, including his conduct with other companies and his level of commercial immorality and incompetence, makes him unfit for the privilege of trading through companies with limited liability (*Re Churchill Hotel* (1987); *Re Dawson Print Group* (1986)).

KEY CASE

RE CHURCHILL HOTEL (1987)

The director had been a director of four companies which had had negligible capital, had borrowed heavily, had traded unprofitably and had become insolvent within a five-year period. Moreover, debts due to the Crown, particularly PAYE tax, had not been paid, but the sums in question used to finance current trading, and there had been non-compliance with the statutory obligation to file accounts. It was held that gross incompetence—even arising other than from commercial immorality, e.g. due to pressure of work—was sufficient for disqualification. On the facts, the judge held that the director's conduct rendered him unfit to be concerned with the management of the company. However, he held that, in exercising his discretion to make a disqualification order under CA 1985 s.300, he should take account of other matters relating to whether it was appropriate to disqualify the director, such as his conduct in (successfully) conducting business as a director of other companies and whether it was unreasonable that such work should be conducted through the medium of limited liability companies. Accordingly no order was made. Now that the discretion to disqualify the director of an insolvent company under CA 1985 s.300 has been replaced by a duty to do so under CDDA 1986 s.6, the order would have to be made. Since the judge distinguished the director's unfitness from his conduct in relation to other companies, this latter factor should not be taken into account in assessing his unfitness. The balancing act performed in *Re Churchill Hotel* may, however, offer guidance as to the exercise of the discretionary powers under CDDA 1986.

RE LO-LINE ELECTRIC (1988)

There were not dissimilar circumstances to those in *Re Churchill Hotel* in *Re Lo-Line Electric* (1988). There, it was acknowledged that disqualification was to protect the public rather than to punish the director but that the interference with the freedom of the individual made the application of natural justice (albeit flexibly) imperative. Ordinary commercial mismanagement short of a lack of commercial probity is not enough. It is, however, not necessary that the director be one *de jure*—the *de facto* performance of the role is sufficient. Yet again, however, there was exhibited a reluctance to exercise the statutory discretion under the repealed CA 1985 s.300. Since the person in question wanted and needed to continue to act in relation to family companies, the judge declined to make the order on the condition that financial and voting control of those companies remained in others. In other words, a general disqualification was not made where the object of the disqualifying power could be otherwise secured.

Relevant factors for **CDDA 1986 s.6** include: deception (*Re Godwin Warren* (1992)); non-payment of Crown debts (the Crown is an involuntary debtor, and employees' benefits may be affected; and it may indicate an intention only to pay creditors who press for payment: *Re Sevenoaks Stationery* (1989)); trading at the risk of creditors, e.g. by not paying creditors who do not press for payment, not taking security and misappropriating money, as well as non-co-operation with insolvency practitioners (*Secretary of State v McTighe (No.2)* (1996)); failure to ensure proper financial accounting (*Re New Generation* (1992)); the level of a director's personal responsibility (*Re Cladrose* (1989)); abdication of responsibility to a co-director and reliance on professional advisers (*Re Bradcrown* (2000)); purchase of the company's stock at a forced-sale value (*Re Keypak* (1989)); and the allotment of shares to himself and his family to maintain control (*Re Looe Fish* (1993)). An individual example of misconduct is sufficient (*SoS v Tighe (No.2)* (1996).

It is no excuse that creditors could or would be paid in full (*Re Normanton Wells* (2010) Ch) or that default is not for the director's personal benefit and even to his personal detriment, though it may produce a lower penalty (*Re Sevenoaks Stationery* (1989)). Failure to resign when the company is trading at the risk of creditors and the directors' advice is unheeded is insufficient per se (*Secretary of State v Gash* (1996)). Evidence of general reputation is not admissible (*Re Dawes & Henderson* (1996)). The director's human rights should be respected (*cf. Re Blackspur (No.3)* (2001), entitling him to relief if proceedings are unreasonably protracted (*Eastaway v UK* (2004) ECtHR; though *cf. Re Blackspur Group (No.4)*, *Eastaway v Secretary of State* (2007) CA) and (*Secretary of State v Doffman* (2010)). Also an application for disqualification may be struck out if the applicant's inordinate delay prejudices the respondent (e.g. where he has been pursuing negotiations to acquire directorships) (*Re Noble Trustees* (1993)). Proceedings for disqualification may be stayed if the director gives a suitable undertaking not to act as a director (*cf. Re Blackspur* (1997)).

Disqualification orders must be registered (**CDDA s.18**).

Consequences of Contravention

If a person acts whilst disqualified under the above **CDDA 1986** provisions, he and the company are criminally liable (**CDDA 1986 ss.13–14**).

Joint and several liability with the company for the debts of the company is incurred by:

(a) a person who acts whilst disqualified by a disqualification order or whilst he is an undischarged bankrupt, and

(b) a person involved in the management of the company who acts on the instructions of (a) without the court's leave (**CDDA 1986 s.15**).

A court's powers to make a compensation order in criminal cases will be restricted by its decision to disqualify a director (which reduces his means to pay such compensation) (*R. v Holmes* (1991)).

Overcoming Disqualification

A disqualified director may be given permission to act as a director of another company on terms specified (e.g. together with an independent chartered accountant: *Re Majestic Recording Studios* (1988)). Failure to comply with conditions imposed exposes the director to personal liability (*Re Brian Sheridan Cars* (1995)). The length of disqualification is in the judge's discretion. He needs to protect the public and deter future misconduct, taking account of, for example, the director's age and state of health, the length of time he has been in jeopardy, whether he has admitted the offence, his general conduct before and after the offence, and disqualification periods for co-directors (*Re Westmid* (1997)).

A disqualified person may apply to become a director of a particular company (**CDDA 1986 s.17**). The court must balance the reasons for disqualification and the risks to the public against the need for the applicant to be a director of the relevant company (*Re Barings (No.4)* (1998); *Re Dawes & Henderson (No.2)* (1999)).

Role of Director

A director may have a contract of service with the company, whether as director and/or in some additional capacity (*Secretary of State v Bottrill* (1999)). But he cannot be an auditor or, if the sole director, the secretary. Prima facie directors must exercise their powers (unless ministerial) personally and collectively but the articles frequently authorise them to create and delegate functions to a managing director, who is appointed directly by the board, to which he is answerable, albeit (like the other directors) his duties are owed to the company. His powers may be on such terms as the board fixes from time to time (as in *Holdsworth v Caddies*, above, p.45) or completely devolved to him until formally revoked by the board, in which case the company will have three distinct organs each with its own sphere of power.

Director's Cessation of Office

A director ceases to hold office if: he resigns; his period of appointment under the articles or his contract terminates (the articles may provide for vacation of office on a request for resignation by co-directors: *Lee v Chou* (1984)); or he is removed under **CA 2006 s.168** (below). He will not necessarily vacate office because of a breach of his contract of employment, a resolution for liquidation, or the appointment of a receiver out of court whose role is not inconsistent with his (*Griffiths v Secretary of State* (1973)). If he does lose office, he may, if so entitled, nevertheless be able to claim damages for wrongful dismissal (a director should not be dismissed summarily without such misconduct as destroys confidence in him and makes his continued employment impracticable (*Jackson v Invicta* (1985)), compensation for unfair dismissal (*Parsons v Albert Parsons* (1979)) or a redundancy payment.

Without a prior resolution of the general meeting, a director's contract of employment may not be for a guaranteed term of over two years (**CA 2006 s.188**).

Without prejudice to any other power of removal which may exist, **CA 2006 ss.168–169** empowers the company by ordinary resolution to remove a director before the expiry of his period of office, notwithstanding anything in the articles or in any agreement with him, so long as the company receives special (at least 28 days') notice of the resolutions, informs the director and circulates any representations he makes. The statutory power cannot be excluded but it may be circumvented.

KEY CASE

BUSHELL V FAITH (1969)
An article tripling the votes on directors' shares on a resolution to remove a director was upheld, because all the Act required was an ordinary resolution. It was silent on how many votes per share there could be. Lord Upjohn suggested that, if the court were to nullify such an article (which Lord Donovan thought necessary in a family company to prevent repercussions from family quarrels in the board room), then votes should in such a case be given to shareholders who otherwise had none.

However, the exercise of the power of removal under **CA 2006 s.168** does not deprive the director of compensation or damages payable to him in respect of the termination of his appointment as director or of any other appointment terminating with that as director (**CA 2006 s.168(5)**).

OFFICE-HOLDERS; INSOLVENCY PRACTITIONERS

A liquidator, provisional liquidator, administrator, administrative receiver or supervisor of a voluntary arrangement approved by a company under **IA 1986 Pt I** must, subject to criminal penalties, be a qualified insolvency practitioner or authorised substitute (**IA 1986 ss.388–389A**). An insolvency practitioner must be an individual authorised by a competent professional body recognised by the Secretary of State, have prescribed security for the performance of his functions in force, and not be an undischarged bankrupt or subject to a disqualification order under **CDDA 1986** (see above, pp.66–71) or a classified mental patient (**IA 1986 s.390**).

RECEIVERS

Debentures often expressly provide that a receiver may be appointed on the occurrence of a specified event rendering the security enforceable. Receivers may also be appointed under an implied power or the court's inherent power. A receiver must generally get in the assets charged and collect any income due on them. He may realise the assets and pay the proceeds in reduction of the amount owed to the debenture-holders. He may also petition for liquidation.

Usually it will be better for the company to continue trading and to appoint a receiver as manager of the company as well.

A receiver and manager of the whole of the company's property (unless there is another receiver of part) appointed by debenture-holders with a floating charge is an administrative receiver with full powers of management and dealing with the company's property.

The mere appointment of a receiver and manager out of court does not automatically terminate the employment of the directors or even prevent them from continuing to act, so long as that is not inconsistent with the powers of the receiver and the interests of the debenture-holders (*Newhart v Co-operative Bank* (1978)). The commencement of winding-up may deprive the receiver of power to bind the company but he may continue to deal with the property securing the debenture (*Sowman v Samuel* (1978)).

A receiver appointed by the court is an officer of the court (*Moss v Whinney* (1912)) and a receiver appointed by debenture-holders is in principle their agent. It is common to provide that a receiver and manager shall be the agent of the company, in which case he can exercise such powers as the directors can normally exercise. Thus, if the directors are not empowered to petition for winding-up, nor can the receiver exercise their powers, unless he is able to do so on another ground (*Re Emmadart* (1979)). Administrative receivers are always agents of the company (**IA 1986 s.44**) and have extensive powers to act on its behalf (**IA 1986 s.42** and **Sch.1**). However, a right to appoint an administrative receiver does not confer "step-in" rights (*Feetum v Levy* (2005) CA).

A receiver is not personally bound by the company's existing contracts. However, he and the company are both liable on contracts made by him, although he may claim an indemnity from the company (**IA 1986 ss.37** and **44**). He owes a duty to all encumbrancers to act in good faith to preserve and realise assets (taking reasonable care to obtain the best price) but is not in breach merely because action in the best interests of his debenture-holders diminishes the security of subsequent encumbrancers (*Downsview Nominees v First City Corp.* (1992)). He also owes an equitable duty to a mortgagor to manage the property with due diligence (*Medforth v Blake* (1999)). However, since they are agents of the company, receivers' acts as such cannot make them liable for the tort of inducing breach of a contract to which the company is a party: e.g. where, contrary to a contract that the company's customers should pay money into the account of their financier ("E"), receivers requested the customers to pay into the company's own account (*Exfinco*, above, p.34).

COMPANY ADMINISTRATION

Under **IA 1986 s.8** and **Sch.7,** an administrator may be appointed by the court, the holder of a floating charge, or the company or its directors, in order (in descending order of importance):

(a) to rescue the company as a going concern;

(b) to achieve a better result for its creditors as a whole than would be likely on liquidation; and/or

(c) to realise property to make a distribution to secured creditors.

Administration Orders

The court has power to make an administration order if:

(a) the company is or is likely to become unable to pay its debts; and

(b) the order would be reasonably likely to achieve the purpose of administration.

The court may approve a "pre-packaged administration", where the details have already been arranged by interested parties, but will be careful to ensure that creditors are not disadvantaged (*Re Halliwells LLP* (2010) Ch).

Effect of Administration

The effect of administration is that:

(a) no steps may be taken with a view to a winding-up;

(b) there may not be in office an administrative receiver (if an adminis-tration order has effect) or receiver (if the administrator decides); and

(c) moratorium: the consent of the administrator or permission of the court (which may be subject to terms) is necessary for:

(i) the enforcement of security, the repossession of hire-purchased goods or a landlord's exercise of his right of forfeiture; or

(ii) enforcement of legal proceedings.

Administrator's Duties

The administrator must:

(a) notify the company, discoverable creditors and the registrar of, and publicise, his appointment;

(b) obtain a statement of the company's affairs;

(c) state his proposals for achieving the purposes of the administration;

(d) arrange creditors' meetings;

(e) take control of company property;

(f) manage the company's affairs, business and property in accordance with approved proposals for achieving the purposes of the administration;

(g) comply with court directions;

(h) take reasonable care to obtain the best price for property disposed of (*Re Charnley Davies (No.2)* (1990)); and

(i) report on the conclusion of the administration.

Administrator's Powers

The administrator may:

(a) do anything for the management of the affairs, business and property of the company;

(b) call meetings of members or creditors;

(c) apply to the court for directions;

(d) make a distribution to creditors;

(e) dispose of charged property (subject to preservation of the secured creditors' rights); and

(f) if sanctioned by the court, dispose of goods subject to a hire-purchase agreement (subject to paying the owner of the goods).

Discharge of the Administrator

The administrator is discharged from office on resignation, removal by the court, ceasing to be qualified as an insolvency practitioner, or discharge of the administration order.

Duties of Directors

14

THE ROLE OF THE DIRECTOR

Individual directors may have different roles in different types of company and it can be misleading to analyse their position solely by reference to familiar broad categorisations. Thus, they act in the capacity of agents, with similar duties but not with all the rights of agents. They may be employed under contract as employees of the company, and be subject to liability both as employee and director (*Simtel v Rebak* (2006); but as directors they have greater obligations of good faith (as may an employee acting as a director: *Helmet v Tunnard* (2006) CA). Their fiduciary position and their position as regards company property liken them to trustees but their duties of care and skill are not as high.

Basically, however, a director must acquire and maintain a sufficient knowledge and understanding of the company's business to enable him properly to discharge his duties (*Re Barings (No.5)* (1998); *Re Vintage Hallmark* (2006)); he is bound to carry out his duties with skill and care; and, in particular, he must act *bona fide* in the interests of the company (particular illustrations of directors' duties largely demonstrate the fiduciary aspects).

Although the duties of directors, along with many other duties, have been governed mainly by the common law, and are as ascertainable as other common law duties, it has long been argued that directors should be able to consult a definitive statement of their obligations. This has now been provided, in CA 2006, s.170 of which purports essentially to reproduce common law and equitable principles and to require the stated principles to be interpreted and applied in the same way as common law and equitable principles but so that they have effect in place of those principles though leaving scope for such principles which have not been put into statutory form!

The stated general duties of directors are:

(a) to act within his powers (in accordance with the company's constitution and only for the purposes for which they are conferred: **CA 2006 s.171**: see above, p.51);

(b) to promote the success of the company (**CA 2006 s.172**);

(c) to exercise independent judgment (**CA 2006 s.173**);

(d) to exercise reasonable, skill, care and diligence (**CA 2006 s.174**);

(e) to avoid conflicts of interest (**CA 2006 s.175**);

(f) not to accept benefits from third parties (**CA 2006 s.176**); and

(g) to declare interest in a proposed transaction or arrangement (**CA 2006 s.177**).

PERFORMANCE OF DUTIES GENERALLY

The statutory and fiduciary obligations of a company director are inescapable personal responsibilities (*Re Westmid* (1997)). In particular, he must exercise independent judgement (**CA 2006 s.173**), though he may take account of his nominator's interests (*Re Neath Rugby Club (No.2)* (2009) CA). A director is under a positive obligation to carry out his duties (albeit they are not generally stated specifically); otherwise an act only capable of being done by directors (*e.g.* transferring shares) cannot be done (*Re Zinotty* (1984)). He must not exceed his powers (**CA 2006 s.171**) (although, if he does, the company may still be bound: see Ch.9); and he must indemnify the company for losses incurred as a result of any breach of duty, as well as accounting to it for benefits received as a consequence of his position as director.

Although directors may delegate functions to those below them in the management chain, they must supervise the discharge of delegated functions (*Re Barings (No.5)* (1998)) and report wrongdoing (*Lexi Holdings v Luqman* (2009) CA), and they must generally not delegate the exercise of their discretion. This they must exercise (*bona fide*) as they (subjectively: *Regentcrest v Cohen* (2000)), and not the court, think fit; nor will the court direct them to exercise discretion in a mandatory way at the instigation of shareholders (*Pergamon v Maxwell* (1970)). However, an agreement between shareholder directors as to how they vote as directors may be valid. And directors may validly enter a binding agreement with third parties if at the time the agreement is made they genuinely believe it to be in the interests of the company (*Fulham FC v Cabra* (1993)).

An important innovation of **CA 2006 s.172** is the stated duty in good faith to promote the success of the company. In one view this simply reproduces the common law duty of loyalty. And the duty is qualified by the director's having to consider: different interests involved (likely long term consequences; company's employees; business relationships with suppliers, customers and others; the community and the environment; the company's reputation for high standards of business conduct; and fairness between company members). But the statutory duty goes beyond stating that, if and when he acts, then he must discharge the duty; it positively requires him to take action to do so.

PROPER PURPOSE

Directors' freedom of deciding how they will exercise their powers is limited by their having to exercise them constitutionally and for the purposes for which they were given (**CA 2006 s.171**). Their decisions will be upheld if, as a matter of construction, they have acted within their powers (*Re Smith & Fawcett* (1942)) and if their main purpose is proper. Thus, a contract effectively distributing capital to directors avoiding the statutory protection of ordinary creditors on winding-up is unenforceable (*MacPherson v European Strategic* (2000)). But directors who are ordinary shareholders may consider their own interests and capitalise dividends with the effect of weakening the position of preference shareholders, provided that, decided objectively, their moving purpose is to benefit the company (*Mills v Mills* (1938)).

Directors are commonly empowered to issue new shares, primarily in order to raise necessary new finance, albeit the need may not be critical at the time of issue (*Harlowe's Nominees v Woodside* (1968)). It would be improper for them to issue shares to weight the voting strength so as to defeat a takeover bid and entrench themselves in office. But such an issue was said in *Hogg v Cramphorn* (1967) to be ratifiable by the general meeting and was in fact subsequently ratified (see too *Bamford v Bamford* (1969)).

KEY CASE

TECK V MILLAR (1973)
Hogg was not followed in *Teck v Millar* (1973), in which an issue of shares to a firm to whom certain management rights had been granted was upheld, although the existing majority shareholder, who had wished to develop the company's properties, thereby lost control. It was, said the British Columbian court, no exception to the rule requiring the directors to act in the company's interests that the majority shareholders should not be deprived of control; the directors could take account of the reputation, policies and experience of anyone seeking to take over the company.

KEY CASE

SMITH V AMPOL (1974)
The Privy Council in *Smith v Ampol* (1974) explained *Teck* on the basis that the directors' decision related to management (who should obtain exploitation rights?) and not control. The allotment of shares in *Ampol* to a company which wanted to make a take-over bid, with the apparently honest intention of raising much-needed finance, was declared

invalid, its effect being to reduce the majority shareholding of two other companies whose take-over bid had been rejected. Directors should not "interfere with that element of the company's constitution which is separate from and set against their powers".

KEY CASE

CRITERION V STRATFORD (2004)

Similarly, in *Criterion v Stratford* (2004), the House of Lords condemned a "poison pill" agreement between Criterion and its joint venture partner, whereby the joint venture partner could require Criterion to buy out its share in the joint venture on terms which were highly favourable to the partner but damaging to Criterion. The arrangement was too wide ranging and on the facts was condemned in respect of a takeover of Criterion. However, the House did not consider the opinion in the lower courts that an exercise of powers to oppose a takeover might be justifiable.

KEY CASE

LEE PANAVISION V LEE LIGHTING (1991)

In *Lee Panavision v Lee Lighting* (1991), the controlling shareholders of Lighting were about to terminate an agreement whereby Lighting was managed by Panavision (to which it was heavily in debt). Lighting's directors (mostly Panavision appointees) resolved to enter a further management agreement with Panavision. They acted in good faith, but they had exercised their powers for an improper purpose—to divert control from Lighting's shareholders (and any directors they might appoint) to Panavision—so the new agreement was unenforceable.

A transaction effected by directors' exercising powers for an improper purpose is voidable by the company and unenforceable by the third party if he has acted "unconscionably" (*Criterion v Stratford* (2004)).

. . . .

LOYALTY

CA 2006 states three duties which may be regarded as aspects of traditional duties of good faith and loyalty, namely: to avoid conflicts of interest (**CA 2006 s.175**); not to accept benefits from third parties (**CA 2006 s.176**); and to declare interest in a proposed transaction or arrangement (**CA 2006 s.177**).

Conflict of Interest

A director should not place himself in a position in which there does or might arise a conflict between his duties to the company and the interests of either himself or a third party (*Bhullar v Bhullar* (2003)). Thus, a director should disclose to the company breach of duty by a fellow director (*British Midland v Midland International* (2003)) or himself (*Item Software v Fassihi* (2004) CA). Also, a director who has a contract of employment with his company should not act as a director of another company, because he must not compete with his company (*Hivac v Park Royal* (1946)). But, where competition is not intended, and the presence of another company's director on the board as a non-executive director not under a contract of service might be a beneficial influence, are multiple directorships justifiable (*cf.* the *London & Mashonaland* case (1891))?

The director's duty may survive his leaving the company (*Foster Bryant v Bryant* (2007) CA) and he may be held liable for the fruits of a corporate opportunity which is realised by him personally or by another company (*CMS Dolphin v Simonet* (2001); *Re Allied Business* (2009) CA). But the non-competition rule depends on the facts, and a director who had been excluded from a company could retain profits from a rival company which he subsequently founded (*In Plus Group v Pyke* (2002)).

Interests in Transactions or Arrangements

Equitable principles have traditionally discouraged directors' contracts with their company or with third parties, even where the company benefits from them. A director who so contracts should account to the company for profits received and might even be dismissed. The company may, but need not, avoid the contract (*Boulting v A.C.T.A.T.* (1963)). **CA 2006 ss.177** and **182** impose a basic duty on a director with an interest of which he is aware in an existing, present or proposed transaction or arrangement with the company to declare the nature of his interest to the other directors. The director of a single director company must disclose to a meeting composed, if necessary, only of himself (*Neptune v Fitzgerald* (1995))!

The extent of the duty is uncertain and apparently limited but non-compliance means: a fine, the contract is voidable, and loss of the protection of an exemption clause, which might otherwise excuse him from liability.

The director's means of avoiding the consequences of breach of the general rule include: disclosure, authorisation or ratification by the general meeting, or a clause in the articles qualifying liability. Such clauses will be given effect according to their terms (*Movitex v Bulfield* (1986)) but are subject to compliance with **CA 2006 ss.177** and **182**, to general adherence to the overriding duty to promote the success of the company (**CA 2006 s.172**) and to the invalidation of any exemption or indemnity in respect of negligence, default, breach of duty or breach of trust (**CA 2006 s.232**).

MOVITEX V BULFIELD (1986)

The articles of the plaintiff company permitted a director to have an interest in a contract made with the company provided that he made full disclosure of his interest. The plaintiff contracted to buy the freehold of certain property but could not raise the finance to pay for it. Two of the plaintiff's directors and shareholders of the defendant company arranged that the defendant company should purchase the property and grant leases of it to the plaintiff. During its winding-up, the plaintiff sought to have the leases set aside as breaching the prohibition against self-dealing by a director. It argued that the articles purporting to excuse the alleged breaches of duty were void by virtue of the CA 1985 s.310 prohibition on provisions which exempt or indemnify a person from or against breach of a duty owed by him to the company. It was held, however, that the relevant articles, having authorised the dealings in question, had provided that such dealings were not, therefore, contrary to the directors' duties. In this case, the relevant duties were excluded, not breached then excused. Therefore, the leases were valid.

If a director of a company or its holding company or a person connected with him enters into a contract for the transfer of a non-cash asset the value of which is at least £5,000 and exceeds £100,000 or 10 per cent of the company's relevant assets, the transaction is generally voidable by the company unless first approved by a resolution in general meeting of the director's company (**CA 2006 ss.190–196**). Unless he took steps to secure compliance with the section or was unaware of contravention, a person contravening it is liable to account for any gain made and to indemnify the company for loss or damage suffered from the transaction (see *Re Duckwari (Nos 1 and 2)* (1998)). A contract made in excess of the directors' powers between the company and a director or person associated with one is voidable, and a director who authorised the transaction is liable to account and to indemnify the company (**CA 2006 s.195**).

Directors' Employment Contracts

Directors' contracts of employment with the company are particularly prescribed, publicity being required of their terms, especially with regard to remuneration. Tax-free payments to directors are banned, as is compensation for (imposed or voluntary) loss of office if not disclosed to and approved by the company (**CA 2006 ss.312–316**). Circumvention of the latter prohibition has been condoned where payments are made in connection with loss of a different office from that of director or if the agreement to compensate ante-dates the loss of office (*Taupo v Rowe* (1977)) but full disclosure should still be necessary.

Substantial Property Transactions, Loans and Credit

Subject to exceptions, a contract for the transfer between a director and the company of a substantial non-cash asset or for a loan or the provision of security or credit by a company to a director or person connected with him is voidable unless approved by a resolution of the members (**CA 2006 ss.190–214**). A director participating in the transaction is liable to make restitution and compensation (*Neville v Krikorian* (2006) CA).

DUTY OF CARE, SKILL AND DILIGENCE

The director's obligation to refrain from negligence has traditionally been treated as light. Several (perhaps not fully convincing) reasons have been given: businessmen are required to take risks and are not to be condemned with hindsight by a judge substituting his own, arguably uninformed, assessment of the circumstances; and directors must be permitted to delegate their functions to other officials. The difficulty of proving that the director's performance would have avoided loss and the loss which would have been avoided narrows the likelihood of litigation to amplify the standard of care.

However, it is now provided, by **CA 2006 s.174**, that a director must exercise reasonable care, skill and diligence, i.e., that which would be exercised by a reasonably diligent person with (a) the (objective) general knowledge, skill and experience that may reasonably be expected of a person carrying out the functions carried out by the director in relation to the company and (b) the (subjective) general knowledge, skill and experience that the director has.

Though the Act is silent on the point, it is probably the case that, subject to the articles and business practice, a reasonable delegation of duties to officials is justified (*Re City Equitable Ins.* (1925), per Romer J.).

BENEFICIARIES OF DIRECTORS' DUTIES

Despite membership of the board of directors and the duties which have to be performed with respect to it (see, e.g. **CA 2006 s.177,** above), a director does not owe his duties to the board itself (i.e. to himself and his fellow directors). Otherwise, directors could sanction their fellows' breach. Duties are not owed to a particular organ of the company (albeit the general meeting may sanction what would otherwise be a breach) but to the company as a whole (i.e. to the shareholders collectively).

Thus, in *Percival v Wright* (above, p.26) directors breached no duty of disclosure to shareholders who had offered them shares at an undervalue (at the time, the stated price was less than the shares were worth, as a higher sum was being offered by a takeover bidder). Their duty to the company required keeping secret confidential negotiations affecting the price. Similarly, *qua* directors, directors owe no duties to shareholders who appoint them, who in turn are not vicariously liable for the acts of directors they appoint (*Kuwait Asia Bank v National Mutual Life* (1990)).

However, so far as a relationship is created on special facts, directors may assume duties to certain shareholders (*Peskin v Anderson* (2000)), e.g. where a director acts as an agent for the sale of particular shareholdings (*Allen v Hyatt* (1914)) or in a small family business (*Coleman v Myers* (1977) NZ). Obligations undertaken by directors directly to shareholders must be properly performed, e.g. advice given must be given in good faith (*Dawson v Coats* (1988)). Likewise, a duty of care may be owed both to shareholders for whom information is provided and to take-over bidders likely to rely on it (*Morgan Crucible v Hill Samuel* (1990)).

Owing duties to the corporate entity means that a director's duty to account for profits survives even though the share-holders at the time of breach of duty have been replaced by new ones who have arguably not suffered from the breach (*Abbey Glen v Stumborg* (1978)).

A fortiori a director appointed by debenture-holders generally owes no duty to them as such. The advantage to them in being able to nominate a director lies in that their nominee can help ensure that company affairs are conducted properly. However, a director's duty to the company may require his taking account of the interests of creditors (*West Mercia Safetywear v Dodd* (1987)).

More direct duties to creditors may be held to exist, at least during winding-up (*Walker v Wimborne* (1978); see too *Re Horsley & Weight*, per Templeman L.J., below, p.85).

KEY CASE

WEST MERCIA SAFETYWEAR V DODD (1987)

A subsidiary and its parent company were in financial difficulties. The parent company's bank overdraft was guaranteed by Dodd, a director of both companies. The month before both companies went into liquidation, Dodd transferred £4,000 from the subsidiary to the parent company. The trial judge held that this was not a breach of the duty owed by Dodd to the subsidiary because the transfer was in part payment of a debt owed by the subsidiary to the parent. However, the Court of Appeal accepted that it was a fraudulent preference, rendering the director liable for misfeasance under IA 1986 s.212. Once a company became insolvent, the interests of its creditors overrode those of its shareholders because at that time the company's assets belonged in a practical sense to the creditors, who had the power to displace the normal powers of the shareholders and of the directors. Accordingly, the director was held personally liable to repay the £4,000, though in the circumstances with an entitlement to a dividend in respect of that sum in the subsidiary's liquidation.

Liability under **IA 1986, s.212** extends to a *de facto* director, and may be strict; but, where a company's sole director is another company, the mere fact that the affairs of the corporate director have to be carried out by its only active human director does not automatically make him a *de facto* director of the first company (*Re Paycheck Services (No.3)* (2010) SC).

The duty to take account of the interests of employees (**CA 2006 s.172(1)(b)**) is not apparently owed other than to the company.

EFFECTS OF BREACH OF DUTY

In addition to possible liability to fines or imprisonment under statute, a director may be liable to summary dismissal (**CA 2006 s.168**).

The company may be able to rescind contracts entered into owing to his breach of duty and it may be able to claim a declaration or an injunction, to restrain breach.

The corollary of the duty not to accept benefits from third parties (**CA 2006 s.176**) is liability to account for that benefit. The rule that a director, whatever his motives, should not keep personal profits which he would, or might, not have made if he had not been a director has traditionally been applied strictly. In *Regal v Gulliver* (1942), directors had to account for profits made on the sale of shares in a subsidiary, as their original opportunity to acquire the shares arose by virtue of their positions as directors, even though they acted in the company's interests and the general meeting would have ratified their actions, given the opportunity (see too *Boardman v Phipps* (1966)). Whether his being unable to profit personally depends on breach of confidence or abuse or misuse of information which is the company's property or on preventing conflict of interest is not clear.

The director will be personally liable to account for benefits received (*Sinclair Investments v Versailles* (2011) CA) and will hold on a constructive trust any property belonging to the company in equity (*JJ Harrison v Harrison* (2001)). In *Ball v Eden Project* (2001) the director had to assign to the company a trade mark obtained in breach of fiduciary duty. Where a managing director outside his authority used company money to bribe third parties for the company's advantage, he was nevertheless held liable to repay it (*Hannibal v Frost* (1987)). A director will be liable to make restitution of the amount of any dividends wrongfully paid out, regardless of the amount of the company's loss (*Bairstow v Queens Moat Houses* (2001)). He may also have to pay compensation or damages. For using company property for his own purposes in breach of his fiduciary duties, a director may also have to pay compound interest on sums he has to pay (*Wallersteiner v Moir (No.2)* (1975)). A claim for restoration of property (and its fruits) is likely to be more advantageous than one for payment of money (*Gwembe Valley v Koshy (No.3)* (2003) CA). Third parties who have participated in the breach may also be liable to damages or an action for money had and received (*Mahesan v Malaysia Housing* (1978)) or to a constructive trust (*Selangor v Cradock (No.3)* (1968)).

Directors may escape liability if the general meeting validly ratifies the breach (unless this amounts to fraud on the minority) or if they can claim an indemnity from the company (or if they are insured). But directors with all the issued shares who commit misfeasance by an act of gross negligence inflicting loss on the creditors may not be able to ratify that gross negligence (*Re Horsley & Weight* (1980), per Templeman L.J.).

The court has a discretion to relieve directors, wholly or in part, from breach of duty committed in their official capacity if they ought in the circumstances to be excused (**CA 2006 s.1157**—though not in the case of wrongful trading: *Re Produce Marketing Consortium* (1989)) but probably only in respect of claims brought by or on behalf of the company (*Customs & Excise v Hedon Alpha* (1981)).

Decision-making

15

Company decisions are basically made by meetings of the shareholders, which may sometimes be attended by others, particularly debenture-holders. However, where a statute or the articles of association require a course of action to be taken by a particular group in accordance with a prescribed procedure, the procedure is generally unnecessary if the group (*Re Duomatic* (1968)) or the shareholders generally (*Euro Brokers v Monecor* (2002)) otherwise agree; but not if such agreement is not valid (*Re RW Peak* (1997)) or, possibly, if it is made by beneficial owners rather than by shareholders who are registered with voting rights (*Domoney v Godinho* (2004); *cf. Re Tulse-sense* (2010)).

MEETINGS

Fundamental decisions concerning the company's activities and future are decided, insofar as the power of decision has not been devolved on the directors, in general meetings of the shareholders. The rules governing meetings vary, notably from implementation in 2009 of the EC Shareholder Rights Directive (2007), facilitating cross-border exercise of voting rights in listed companies and making special provisions for traded companies (i.e. ones whose shares rights to vote at general meetings and who are admitted to trading on a regulated market in an EEA State by or with the company's consent: **CA 2006 s.360C**) and for the electronic dissemination of information. Usually meetings are confined to the single annual general meeting (AGM). Public companies and traded companies must hold an AGM within six months of the end of its accounting reference date (financial year) (**CA 2006 s.336**) for declaring dividends, considering accounts and the reports of auditors and directors, and for electing directors and auditors. Extraordinary general meetings may be called when the need arises. Meetings of a particular class of members or creditors are called class meetings.

RESOLUTIONS

Decisions in meetings are made by resolution. An ordinary resolution (passed by a simple majority of votes cast by those present and entitled to vote: **CA 2006 s.282**) generally suffices. More important issues may have to be decided by special resolution (requiring a 75 per cent majority of votes cast: **CA 2006 s.283**).

CALLING MEETINGS

The articles can confer or abrogate a right to call meetings. Directors are generally empowered to decide when to call them. But members holding 10 per cent or more of the paid-up capital with voting rights who state their objects may require the directors to call an extraordinary general meeting; if the directors default, it may be convened by requisitionists representing 5 per cent or more of the voting rights (**CA 2006 ss.303–305**). In addition to its inherent power to call meetings, the court may order one to be held and conducted in whatever manner it sees fit where it is otherwise impracticable to call one or conduct it in the prescribed manner (**CA 2006 s.306**); but this does not empower the court to resolve a deadlock at a board or general meeting (*Ross v Telford* (1997)). An auditor may requisition an extraordinary general meeting to consider the circumstances of his resignation (**CA 2006 s.513**).

The articles can determine the necessary period of notice. Each member must generally receive 14 days' notice, 21 days for the AGM or of a special resolution, but general acquiescence may validate a shorter period (**CA 2006 ss.307-307A**). Notice is generally adequate if it enables a member to decide whether he ought to attend to safeguard his interests. It must indicate the time and place and, if pertinent, that it is the AGM or that a special resolution is to be passed. Special notice must be given 28 days before the meeting to the company (which must notify the members: **CA 2006 s.312**) of a resolution to remove a director or, sometimes, of the appointment or removal of an auditor. An individual member cannot use this procedure merely to compel the inclusion of a resolution on the agenda (*Pedley v IWA* (1977)).

A sufficient proportion of members may require the company to circulate those entitled to receive notice of the AGM regarding a resolution to be moved at a meeting (**CA 2006 ss.314–317**). But the directors have the whip hand with circulars as they generally have better opportunity to prepare them and to finance their circulation from company funds. Although participation in voting must generally be by attendance at the meeting, attendance may be by proxies. These are generally influenced by the directors, sending forms of appointment with the circulars representing their views. Even in the case of two-way proxies (required by the Stock Exchange for quoted companies and permitting authorisation to vote either way) members generally authorise proxies to vote with the directors.

THE MEETING

The meeting (which should be quorate—the articles usually allow a small quorum) has as chairman a person elected by the members, generally the managing director or another director.

Unless the specific form of a resolution is pre-determined in the notice of the meeting, a member may move any resolution on the subject-matter indicated in that notice. Members may speak to the motion or any permissible amendment, after which a vote is taken. A show of hands (on which proxies cannot vote), with one vote per person voting, may decide the issue. But a poll can be demanded by a specified number of shareholders (**CA 2006 s.321**) or by the chairman, exercising his power to give effect to the true sense of the meeting. On a poll, each share generally carries one vote, but a member is not obliged to cast all his votes or to cast all those he does use the same way; hence, a nominee shareholder can give effect to the wishes of different beneficial owners.

RESULTS OF MEETING

The company must keep minutes of the meeting and these may be inspected by the members (**CA 2006 ss.355–359**). Resolutions and agreements affecting the company's constitution must be registered, as part of the company's public documents (**CA 2006 ss.29–30**). They include special resolutions and resolutions binding particular classes of shareholders.

Normally, a resolution will be invalidated by non-compliance with the rules governing the conduct of meetings unless all members entitled to vote unanimously assent to the relevant decision (*Re Duomatic* (1969); *EIC Services v Phipps* (2003)) or non-assenting members attend the meeting and acquiesce (*Re Bailey Hay* (1971)) or the result would be the same if the proper procedure were followed (*Bentley-Stevens v Jones* (1974)).

Company and Shareholder Proceedings; Majority Rule

16

At root, company decisions are taken by the members, meeting together and deciding by a majority vote, however large that majority may have to be for a particular issue (see Chapter 15). The members may, and generally do, devolve the power of decision to the board of directors, in which case they may positively have to take it back again before they can exercise it themselves (see Chapter 13). Again, however, it is the members deciding by a majority whether their power is to be devolved or reclaimed. Generally speaking, this practice makes sense. Decisions have to be made some way and it seems fair that the wishes of the majority should prevail (albeit "majority" is generally determined by the number of shares held rather than the number of shareholders voting).

The Rule in *Foss v Harbottle*

Majority rule and the existence of the company's separate legal personality produce an important consequence.

KEY CASE

FOSS V HARBOTTLE (1843)
The directors were alleged to have misapplied company property. Two shareholders wished to bring an action to make them account to the company. But they could not: the company, as the victim of the alleged misconduct, was the proper person to decide whether to sue.

Likewise, in *Mozley v Alston* (1847), shareholders were refused an injunction to restrain allegedly improperly appointed directors from acting—if the majority wished to take action, they should do so through the company. The continuing availability of the majority to decide the point prima facie justifies denial of interference by the minority (*Macdougall v Gardiner* (1875)).

However, although the rule reasonably excluded individual action where the majority were acting legitimately, per se it deprived an individual shareholder of recourse against unreasonable action. Accordingly, in

89

Edwards v Halliwell (1950), certain exceptions to the rule in *Foss v Harbottle* were noted:

(a) It did not apply to ultra vires acts, which by their nature could not be ratified by the majority (see now Chapter 9).

(b) Minority shareholders can complain of a fraud on the minority (see below).

(c) A bare majority cannot do something needing a larger majority.

(d) Individual members can always assert their personal rights.

More recently, **CA 2006 s.994** has provided a remedy for unfair prejudice (see Chapter 19). More significantly, however, rule by majority decision by shareholders under *Foss v Harbottle* can now be overcome by resort to the court under the derivative claims procedure under **CA 2006 s.260** (below).

PERSONAL RIGHTS

It has been argued that every member has a right to have the company's affairs conducted in accordance with the regulations binding himself, the other members and the company by virtue of **CA 2006 s.33**. Certainly he has a right to a personal action if his personal rights are infringed (e.g. to restrain action on the basis of a resolution regarding which his vote is not recorded: *Pender v Lushington* (1877)) or as beneficiary of shares held on trust by a director in breach of trust (*Shaker v Al-Bedrawi* (2002)). But basically his right as a member is to participate in decisions ultimately made by the majority, so that shareholders may be restrained from legal action, in order to give the general meeting the opportunity to decide (*Hogg v Cramphorn* (1966)). A shareholder cannot normally sue personally for a loss reflecting that suffered by the company (*Johnson v Gore Wood*, 2000; *Webster v Sandersons* (2009) CA), even if the defendant has a defence against the company but not against him (*Day v Cook* (2001)); this principle may deprive employees or creditors of a claim. they could pursue if they were not also shareholders (*Gardner v Parker* (2004) CA). Thus, a 50 per cent shareholder and sole director could not sue the other 50 per cent shareholder for diminution in share value—his loss would be remedied if the company successfully sued (*Stein v Blake (No.2)* (1997)). However, the shareholder may sue personally for "reflective loss" where the defendant's wrongful act prevented the company's action (*Giles v Rhind* (2002)).

DERIVATIVE CLAIMS AND PROCEEDINGS

The Pre-existing Law

Provided a decision not to sue has not been made by a majority (independent of any potential defendants) of a competent company organ, individual shareholders may bring a representative or derivative action in respect of a complaint in their capacity as members of the company (the real claimant) where those in control of the company are allegedly at fault (*Atwool v Merryweather* (1867)).

KEY CASE

ATWOOL V MERRYWEATHER (1867)

Atwool v Merryweather involved an attempt to rescind a sale of mines to the company under a transaction whereby the vendors allegedly made a secret profit. Atwool filed a bill in the name of the company as plaintiff but this was declared incompetent because a majority of the shareholders opposed it. He was, however, permitted to proceed with the present action, brought in derivative form on behalf of himself and all of the other shareholders in the company. Discounting the votes of the alleged wrongdoers, a majority of the shareholders supported him.

A representative action is possible where: each member of the class on behalf of whom the action is brought has a separate cause of action; the action will not increase their rights; they share an "interest"; it is for the benefit of the class that the claimant be permitted to sue in a representative capacity (*Prudential v Newman* (1979)); the action is not brought for an ulterior purpose and there is not a better alternative remedy (e.g. putting the company into liquidation) (*Barrett v Ducker*, 1994; *Portfolios of Distinction v Laird* (2004)). The company itself should be made a party to the proceedings so as to be bound by the judgment.

The claimants should first seek a Master's sanction for the proceedings, to secure their right to an indemnity from the company for costs (*Wallersteiner v Moir (No.2)* (1975)). Then, the judge must determine as a preliminary issue that the claimants are entitled to bring a derivative action and that they have established a *prima facie* case that the company is entitled to the relief claimed and that the action falls within the proper boundaries of the *Foss* exception (*Prudential v Newman (No.2)* (1981)). The "injustice of the case" does not found the exception, though it may justify its exercise. In *Estmanco v GLC* (1981), the purchaser of one of a block of flats, and so the holder of a non-voting share in the managing company, was entitled to continue the company's action against the majority shareholder with all the voting shares, which had voted to discontinue the purpose of selling off the remaining flats and finally transferring voting power to the purchasers. Any defence is available which could have been raised against the defendant suing personally, e.g. inequitable conduct (*Nurcombe v Nurcombe* (1984)).

Often such an action will be brought against directors for breach of fiduciary duty. Possibly, a derivative action for negligence cannot lie (*Pavlides v Jensen* (1956)). The contrary has been suggested in view of *Daniels v Daniels* (1978), where minority shareholders successfully pleaded breach of duty by directors and majority shareholders who sold company property to a director's wife at an under-value. But the case has been regarded merely as concerning the obtaining of a personal advantage from the position of the directors, as a fraud on the minority.

A claimant who brings a properly founded derivative action on the above principles may nevertheless be properly prevented from prosecuting the action if that is the corporate will of the company as expressed by an appropriate independent organ (*Smith v Croft (No.3)* (1986)). The appropriate independent organ will vary according to the constitution of the company and the identity of the defendant. In the case of a fraud on the minority, the court could consider the attitude of the majority of shareholders not supporting or likely to support the wrongdoers (*Smith v Croft (No.3)*).

KEY CASE

SMITH V CROFT (NO.3)
The plaintiffs were shareholders with 11.86 per cent of the voting rights. 62.54 per cent of the votes were held by the defendants: namely, the executive directors, companies associated with the executive directors, and the chairman of the company (who was nominated by a company called Wren). Wren held shares carrying 19.66 per cent of the voting rights. The plaintiffs brought a minority shareholders' action to recover money allegedly paid away improperly. They were supported by holders of another 2.54 per cent of the company's shares but opposed by Wren plus other members with shares carrying 3.22 per cent of the votes. It was held that the plaintiffs had no indefeasible right to prosecute a minority shareholders' action. It was proper to have regard to the views of the independent shareholders. Their votes should only be disregarded if, or if there were a substantial risk that, they would be cast in order to support the defendant directors rather than for the benefit of the company. There being no evidence of that and it being clear that the majority of shareholders other than the plaintiffs were opposed to the action, it was struck out. Should it be necessary in such a case to

examine whether the "independent" shareholders (the largest of whom, after all, had nominated one of the defendants) were voting in the interests of the company or sufficient to ask whether they were exercising their rights in their own selfish interests (other than simply for the purpose of supporting the defendants)?

CA 2006 s.260 Derivative Claims

In practice, since derivative claims are likely to be provoked by acts of directors, the pre-existing provision for derivative claims will be displaced by the procedure enacted in **CA 2006 ss.260–264**. Thus, under **ss.260–265** or under the unfair prejudice procedure in **s.994** (below, Chapter 19), an application may be made to the court to bring a derivative action against the director (or other person or both) where:

(i)   a member of a company applies to bring proceedings

(ii)   against a director (or another person or both),

(iii)   in respect of a cause of action arising from the actual or proposed act or omission involving negligence, default, breach of duty or breach of trust by a director,

(iv)   the cause of action is vested in the company,

(v)   and relief is sought on behalf of the company.

For a claim to proceed: it should be consistent with the director's duty to promote the success of the company under **CA 2006 s.172** (*Franbar Holdings v Patel* (2009)); the applicant must make out a prima facie case, then the court must decide that there is a sufficiently strong case that a director was at fault (*Iesini v Westrip* (2009)). The court may then: give permission to continue the claim on terms it thinks fit; refuse permission and dismiss the claim; or adjourn proceedings and give such directions as it thinks fit.

. . . .

VOTING AND FRAUD ON THE MINORITY

A shareholder is generally free to exercise his vote as he wishes. Thus, in *North West Transportation v Beatty* (1887), a member could participate in the company's ratification of a contract with him which was voidable because he also held a position as director. In *Northern Counties v Jackson & Steeple* (1974), a director was bound, by his duty to the company, to call a meeting and to recommend a particular resolution which the company had to pass, or be in contempt of court: but as a shareholder he was entitled to vote against it. Also, if he wishes, a shareholder may contract to exercise his vote in a particular way. Thus, although the company is conventionally regarded as unable to restrict its statutory power to alter its articles or restructure its capital, an agreement between shareholders as to how they will vote on such a proposal can be enforced (*Russell v Northern Bank* (1992)).

However, the fact that the company is merely the object of the free collective will exercised by the members does not mean that there are no restraints *inter se* on their voting.

First, it is now provided that the ratification by a company of conduct by a director amounting to negligence, default, breach of duty or breach of trust can only be ratified by a resolution of members of the company, excluding the director and "any member connected with him" (**CA 2006 s.239**).

Secondly, a shareholder may be injuncted against voting manifestly contrary to the interests of the company (e.g. to prevent essential financial restructuring) or of a lender (where failure to restructure would seriously diminish the assets) *via* which it expected repayment (*Standard Chartered Bank v Walker* (1991)). Minority shareholders can restrain the majority from depriving the company of property it owns or advantages owed to it, such as the opportunity of particular contracts (*Menier v Hooper's Telegraph* (1874); *Cook v Deeks* (1916)). Thirdly, the general meeting cannot generally relieve directors of liability for impending or past breaches of duty except where it is apprised of the full facts and acts *bona fide* in the interests of the company (*Hogg v Cramphorn* (1966); *Bamford v Bamford* (1969)). Thus, it cannot authorise or ratify "fraudulent" conduct (*Atwool v Merryweather* (1867)).

Fourthly, the majority can be restrained from altering the articles of association to buy out the minority where they are merely acting to further their own capricious interests (*Dafen v Llanelly* (1907); *Brown v British Abrasive Wheel* (1919)). But the court is not entitled to prevent the majority's action if it cannot otherwise be shown not to be *bona fide* in the company's interests (*Sidebottom v Kershaw* (1920); *Shuttleworth v Cox* (1927)). When is a variation of class rights permissible? If it is in the interests of an individual hypothetical member (in which case do shareholders owe any duties to the other members)? Or so long as there is no discrimination against minorities (arguably the result of any majority decision)? Does the "contract of membership" under **CA 2006 s.33** confer duties as well as rights?

KEY CASE

CLEMENS V CLEMENS (1976)

A 55 per cent shareholder voted for an alteration of the memorandum which would permit the introduction of a share incentive scheme for employees and would simultaneously reduce her niece's 45 per cent shareholding to 25 per cent. The judge set the resolution aside on the basis that the majority shareholder's aim was to prevent her niece's ever gaining control (by exercising her right of pre-emption) and that shareholders' rights are subject to equitable considerations which may make it unjust to exercise them in a particular way. If this is true, to what extent can such a consideration be applied to companies with a larger, more diverse, membership?

Publicity

17

GENERAL PROVISIONS

English company law persistently requires disclosure of certain details, whether to the public or to particular individuals or groups of individuals, so that persons have sufficient information to enable them to decide whether to act or refrain from acting in a particular way or to verify whether they are doing so. For example, prospectuses inducing persons to become shareholders must apprise potential subscribers of certain facts (see Chapter 3).

Information may be made available in different ways to different individuals. A company could publicise as many details about its affairs as it wishes but, like most natural persons, it will prefer to keep them private. If it wishes its shares to be listed on the Stock Exchange, it will have to undertake to provide the Exchange with information which can be made generally available.

Lower minimal standards are currently laid down by the law, which requires specified matters to be registered and made open to public inspection, e.g. the memorandum, the articles, special resolutions, names of officers, and details of share capital and notifiable interests in shares. Companies must generally make annual returns to the Registrar (**CA 2006 ss.854-859**), though this is relaxed where it trades on a relevant market and is thereby subject to disclosure requirements (**s.856B**). In addition, the Registrar must gazette notice of certain documents he issues or registers: e.g. a certificate of incorporation, notification of alteration of the constitution or of the directors and a copy of a winding-up order (**CA 2006 ss.1064, 1078**). Other information must be maintained by the company, e.g. the minutes of meetings. Some of this information may be inspected by the public (normally, the information that is also available at the Companies Registry), some by the members (e.g. minutes of general meetings) and some only by the directors (e.g. books of account). But a right of inspection may be restricted. A director may inspect accounts to carry out his duties as director (*Oxford Legal Group v Sibbasbridge* (2008) CA); but the court may refuse to allow him to exercise his right, which he holds for the benefit of the company, where it would be injurious to the company (*Conway v Petronius* (1978)).

CONWAY V PETRONIUS (1978)
The directors of a clothing company applied for inspection of the books of the company and of its parent company and to take copies, ostensibly with a view to investigate misapplication of assets. The defendants (the two companies and directors thereof) opposed this on the grounds that the plaintiffs were seeking to solicit information which would be of use to the clothing company and that a general meeting of that company had been called which would consider a resolution to remove the plaintiffs as directors. The court held that it had a discretion to order inspection, which it would not normally withhold where it was sought by a director seeking to exercise his right in the interests of the company and there was no likelihood of his being removed from office. However, where there was evidence of lack of confidence in a director by the convening of a meeting to remove him from office, the court was said to be likely to postpone making an order for inspection until after such meeting unless it were necessary for the protection of the company or for the personal protection of the director.

Bare information may be of little use except to those with professional advisers able to assess and explain its significance. In such cases, another source of publicity, the financial press, may play a useful role in exposing facets of a company's dealings. This may well be so with the details of company accounts and auditors, many of the current requirements for which are regulated by EU law.

Accounts

The directors must (**CA 2006 s.394**), in respect of each accounting reference period, prepare a profit and loss account and a balance sheet (both of which must give a true and fair view of the company's affairs at the end of its financial year). The accounts, which must disclose substantial contracts (for remuneration and other benefits) with directors (**CA 2006 ss.412–413**), must comply with formal and substantive requirements; however, small companies are entitled to exemptions (**CA 2006 ss.381–384**). The accounts must be accompanied by a directors' report (on the company's principal activities during the year, stating the recommended dividend and containing a fair *business review* of the company's performance and of the risks facing it) (**CA 2006 ss.415–419**) and the auditors' report (**CA 2006 ss.495–497**).

As well as preparing "individual accounts", directors of parent companies must also (subject to certain exceptions) prepare "group accounts" (**CA 2006 ss.398–408**). The accounts should be sent to the members, then laid before the general meeting; copies must be delivered to the Registrar. However, summary financial statements are permissible in accordance with regulations made by the Secretary of State (**CA 2006 s.426**). Accounting records must also be kept at the company's offices (**CA 2006 ss.386–389**). The duty of care of a person preparing company accounts is generally owed to the company, not to third parties (e.g. take-over bidders), unless the auditor assumes a duty to the third party (*Abbot v Strong* (1998)).

Auditors

The accuracy of the accounts must be verified by independent auditors (who are generally accountants), appointed by the general meeting (**CA 2006 ss.485–491**), thereby becoming officers of the company (*Mutual Reinsurance v Peat Marwick* (1996)).

An individual or a firm may be appointed as an auditor of a company if he is a member of a recognised supervisory body, is eligible for appointment under the rules of that body, and has a sufficient degree of independence from that company (**CA 2006 ss.1212–1215**). The Secretary of State is empowered to make regulations for the registration of auditors and for requiring recognised supervisory bodies to make available to the public information about firms eligible for appointment as company auditors (**CA 2006 ss.1239–1240**).

Auditors must examine the accounts (**CA 2006 s.495**) and are empowered to obtain necessary information for that purpose and attend company meetings (**CA 2006 ss.499–502**). They must decide whether proper accounting records have been kept, whether proper returns adequate for their audit have been received from branches not visited by them, and whether the companies' individual accounts agree with the accounting records and returns (**CA 2006 s.498**).

In their report, which must be signed, the auditors must state whether in their opinion the accounts have been properly prepared and, in particular, whether a true and fair view has been given of the state of affairs at the end of, and the profit and loss during, the financial year; and also (if the case) whether the information given in the directors' report is consistent with the accounts (**CA 1985 ss.495–497**). In carrying out and reporting on his audit, an auditor owes a duty of reasonable care to the company and possibly to its holding company (*Barings v Coopers & Lybrand* (1996); *Equitable Life v Ernst & Young* (2003) CA; *Stone & Rolls v Moore Stephens* (2009) HL) but generally not to individual shareholders or to potential investors (*Caparo v Dickman* (1990)) unless he knows that a third party may rely on the accounts (*Morgan Crucible v Hill Samuel* (1990); *Galoo v Bright Grahame Murray* (1993)). Liability depends upon an assumption of responsibility to the claimant (*Caparo v Dickman* (1990)), which need not occur consciously (*Electra v KPMG* (1999)).

If auditors discover serious wrongdoing, they should not wait until they report but should immediately inform management or, if the management is involved, a third party (*Sasea v KPMG* (1999)).

An auditor may be removed by ordinary resolution, though without prejudice to his rights to attend and address the general meeting or to damages (**CA 2006 s.510**). If he resigns, he must state whether or not this is because of circumstances of which the members should know (**CA 2006 s.519**). If it is, he may requisition an extraordinary general meeting to receive and consider his explanations (**CA 2006 s.518**).

INSPECTIONS, INVESTIGATIONS AND EXAMINATIONS

The Secretary of State may require the production of specified company documents (**CA 1985 s.447**). He can also appoint an investigator to investigate and report on the company's affairs where it appears there are circumstances suggesting that its business has been or is being conducted fraudulently or oppressively, or that officers have been guilty of misconduct or members have not been given information they are entitled to expect (**CA 1985 s.432**). The company and the members may be able to require or request an investigation but they normally invite the Secretary of State to decide. He is also empowered to investigate the company's ownership.

The threat of an investigation may deter undesirable conduct, but the appointment of an inspector supposedly carries no adverse implication, so he is not bound by the rules of natural justice (*Norwest v DTI* (1978)), although he must act fairly (*Re Pergamon* (1970)). The inspector may inform the Secretary of State of suspected offences and he must report to the Secretary of State, who may bring civil proceedings on behalf of the company (**CA 1985 s.438**) or petition for a winding-up in the public interest (IA 1986 s.124A) or for relief against unfair prejudice under CA 2006 Pt 30 (Chapter 19). The Secretary of State may also assist overseas regulatory authorities by requiring the production of documents and provision of information (CA 1989 ss.82–89).

These legal powers underpin the system of regulation provided by the Stock Exchange, the City Panel and the Financial Services Authority (see especially **FSMA 2000 s.169**).

A liquidator, receiver or administrator may apply to the court for private examination of: a company officer, someone suspected of possession of company property or of being the company's debtor, or any person capable of giving information about the company's affairs (**IA 1986 s.236**). The court has a general discretion whether to make the order, balancing the reasonable requirements of the office-holder in discharging his functions against the need to avoid making an order which is unreasonable, unnecessary or oppressive (*British & Commonwealth v Spicer & Oppenheim* (1992)). An examinee is not entitled to privilege against self-incrimination (*Bishopsgate v Maxwell* (1992)). Use of the transcript of the examination in evidence in legal proceedings is admissible subject to non-infringement of the examinee's human rights (*cf. Saunders v United Kingdom* (1996) ECtHR). Compelled evidence may not normally be used in criminal proceedings (*R. v Secretary of State Ex p. McCormick* (1998)) but may be used for disqualification proceedings (*Re Pantmaenog* (2003) HL).

Liquidations

18

Although winding-up (or liquidation) may be carried out other than in cases of insolvency, the main statutory provisions are consolidated in the Insolvency Act 1986. A company may be considered insolvent if it is unable to pay its debts as they fall due or if its liabilities exceed its assets (see *BNY v Eurosail* (2011) CA). This is supported by detailed Insolvency Rules made by the Insolvency Rules Committee (**IA 1986 ss.411–412**). Liquidation may be either compulsory or voluntary.

COMPULSORY LIQUIDATION

The court may be petitioned by:
- (a) the company;
- (b) any creditor who establishes a prima facie case;
- (c) ontributories (those shareholders who may contribute to the company's assets on liquidation: **IA 1986 ss.74, 79**);
- (d) the Secretary of State; or
- (e) the Official Receiver (an official appointed to that office by the Secretary of State and who is an officer of the court) (**IA 1986 s.124**).

Grounds

The grounds are that:
- (a) the company has so resolved;
- (b) it was incorporated as a public company and has not been issued with a trading certificate within 12 months of registration;
- (c) it is an "old public company" (i.e. one that has not reregistered as a public company or become a private company under the current legislation);
- (d) it has not commenced business within a year of incorporation or has not carried on business for a year;
- (e) the number of members has fallen below the statutory minimum;
- (f) it is unable to pay its debts; or
- (g) it is just and equitable to wind it up (**IA 1986 s.122**).

An order will not be made if the real purpose of the application is other than for winding-up, e.g. to enforce a debt (*Stonegate v Gregory* (1979)).

The "just and equitable" ground enables the court to subject the exercise of legal rights to equitable considerations. It can take account of personal relationships of mutual trust and confidence in small companies, particularly where there is breach of an understanding that all members may participate in the business (*Ebrahimi v Westbourne Galleries* (1972)) or of an implied obligation to participate in management (*Tay Bok Choon v Tahansan* (1987)).

KEY CASE

EBRAHIMI V WESTBOURNE GALLERIES (1972)

Two partners turned their partnership into a company of which they were equal shareholders and partners until the son of one of them joined the company as a shareholder and director. In time, after a disagreement, the father and son removed the other director from the board. It was held that he was entitled to relief by means of an order to have the company wound up on the "just and equitable" ground.

An order may similarly be made where the majority deprive the minority of their right to appoint and remove their own director (*Re A & BC Chewing Gum* (1975)). A member of a company set up as a joint venture may petition even though the agreement between the parties to the venture expressly stated that it was not to be a partnership (*Re A Company (No.003028 of 1987)* (1987)).

KEY CASE

RE A COMPANY (NO.00370 OF 1987) EX P. GLOSSOP (1988)

The petitioner complained that the directors of a family company had given inadequate consideration to what proportion of the profits should have been recommended for distribution by way of dividend. Harman J. said that, subject to ensuring that the company was not trading in a risky fashion and had adequate reserves for its business, trading profits ought to be distributed by way of dividend. Even if profits were being accumulated for the benefit of members, a petition for winding-up on the "just and equitable" ground could be presented if the legitimate expectations of the members were not fulfilled.

Once liquidation begins, generally when the petition is presented (**IA 1986 s.129**), dispositions of company property generally become void (**IA**

1986 s.127) and litigation involving the company is generally restrained (**IA 1986 s.130**).

The court may dismiss the petition or make a winding-up order (**IA 1986 s.125**). It can do so if the petitioner unreasonably refrains from an alternative course of action (*Re A Company* (1983)). It is empowered to appoint an official receiver and one or more liquidators and has general powers to enable rights and liabilities of claimants and contributories to be settled. Separate meetings of creditors and contributories may decide to nominate a person for the appointment of liquidator and possibly of a supervisory liquidation committee (of their representatives) to act with him (**IA 1986 s.141**).

VOLUNTARY LIQUIDATION

Voluntary liquidation begins when the company so resolves, whence it generally ceases to carry on business (**IA 1986 ss.84–88**). If the directors have previously made a declaration of the company's solvency, it is a members' voluntary winding-up (**IA 1986 s.90**): in that case, the general meeting appoints the liquidators (**IA 1986 s.91**). If not, it is a creditors' voluntary winding-up (**IA 1986 s.90**); if so, a meeting of creditors must be called, to which the directors must report on the company's affairs (**IA 1986 ss.98–99**).

In the case of a members' voluntary winding-up, a liquidator must be appointed (**IA 1986 s.91**). In the case of a creditors' voluntary winding-up, a liquidator and a liquidation committee may be appointed (**IA 1986 ss.100–101**).

Though a voluntary winding-up of a company has begun, a compulsory liquidation order is still possible, but a petitioning contributory would need to satisfy the court that a voluntary liquidation would prejudice the contributories (**IA 1986 s.116**).

LIQUIDATORS

Powers and Duties
The powers commonly and potentially available to a liquidator during a winding-up are collected in **IA 1986 Sch.4**. Certain powers are exercisable without sanction; others require sanction, either by the court, an extraordinary resolution (in a members' voluntary winding-up) or the liquidation committee or a meeting of the company's creditors (in a creditors' voluntary winding-up) (**IA 1986 ss.165–168**).

With sanction, he may pay creditors and make compromises or

arrangements with creditors. Without sanction (unless it is a compulsory winding-up), he may carry on legal proceedings and carry on the business of the company so far as may be necessary for its beneficial winding-up.

Without sanction, he may *inter alia* sell company property, claim against insolvent contributories, raise money on the security of company assets, and do all such things as may be necessary for the company's winding-up and distribution of assets. However, he cannot enter into a champertous agreement to assign the fruits of an action against the directors for wrongful trading to a third party offering to finance the litigation (*Re Oasis Merchandising* (1996)).

In a compulsory liquidation, the liquidator must assume control of all property to which the company appears to be entitled (**IA 1986 s.144**). The exercise of his powers is subject to the supervision of the court. He may summon meetings of creditors and contributories and may be compelled to do so by one-tenth in value of them (**IA 1986 s.168**).

In a voluntary winding-up, the liquidator may exercise the court's power of settling a list of contributories and of making calls, and he may summon general meetings of the company for any purpose he thinks fit (**IA 1986 s.165**). In a creditors' voluntary winding-up, he must report to the creditors' meeting on the exercise of his powers (**IA 1986 s.166**).

The liquidator is generally obliged to make returns and accounts (**IA 1986 s.170**), owes fiduciary duties to the company and should investigate the causes of the company's failure and the conduct of its managers, in the wider public interest of action being taken against those engaged in commercially culpable conduct (*Re Pantmaenog* (2003)).

Depending upon the type of liquidation, he may be removed by the court, by a general meeting of the members or by a general meeting of the creditors (**IA 1986 ss.171–172**).

Under **IA 1986 s.108(2)**, the court may remove a liquidator and appoint another if there is "cause shown", by the applicant for his removal, why this should be done. It is not necessary to demonstrate personal misconduct or unfitness for this purpose. It will, however, be enough if the liquidator fails to display sufficient vigour in the discharge of his duties, for instance, by not establishing the current assets and recent trading of the company or in not attempting to secure as favourable as possible terms for the company in, e.g. the disposal of its assets (*Re Keypak Homecare* (1987)). A liquidator who is appointed to wind up a failing business should act with professional efficiency and not exercise the sort of complacency that might have caused the business to decline in the first place.

PRIORITY OF CLAIMS

Property which is in the possession of a company but is in fact owned by someone else (e.g. the supplier under an effective retention of title clause: see above, p.34) is not part of the company's assets and should, therefore, be redelivered to its owner and not retained subject to the claims of company creditors. However, a remedial constructive trust will not be recognised over property which has already become subject to the insolvency regime (*Re Polly Peck* (1998)).

Before claims are met, creditors are entitled to enforce their secured claims against company property subject to fixed charges to the extent their claims may be so met: thereafter, they rank as unsecured creditors. A purchaser of land can normally obtain specific performance, as it is unfair to deprive him of a proprietary right (*Re Coregrange* (1984)).

The costs of liquidation must be met first out of the company's remaining assets.

Next rank, *pari passu*, certain preferential payments (**IA 1986 ss.175, 386** and **Sch.6**), i.e.:

(a) occupational pension scheme contributions;
(b) remuneration owed to employees for the preceding four months (subject to any limits set by the Secretary of State) and accrued holiday remuneration.

Claims of persons who have distrained goods within the preceding three months are postponed to the preferential creditors (**IA 1986 s.176**).

A prescribed part of the company's net property must normally be made available to satisfy the claims of unsecured creditors (**IA 1986 s.176A**), and the expenses of winding-up must be paid (**IA 1986 s.176ZA**), before the claims of floating chargees are satisfied. The unsecured creditors' fund is: 50 per cent of property worth up to £10,000; and 20 per cent of further property; up to a maximum of £600,000 (**SI 2003/2097**).

Then the claims of debenture holders secured by floating charges are paid (**IA 1986 ss.40, 175**).

Remaining unsecured claims (so far as not satisfied by the unsecured creditors' fund) provable in insolvency are then paid pari passu. This includes claims qua purchasers of shares by claimants who have become members (*Soden v British & Commonwealth Holdings* (1997)).

All remaining debts are then paid.

Finally, the company's assets are divided amongst the members according to their rights (in the articles) on liquidation.

No provision is necessary for untraced shareholders (*Re Electricidad*

(1978)). Unclaimed assets vest in the Crown as *bona vacantia* (**CA 2006 s.1012**: see too **CA 2006 ss.1013–1014**).

DISSOLUTION

Having wound up the company's affairs, the liquidator must call a final meeting of the members (if it is a members' voluntary winding-up: **IA 1986 s.194**), the creditors (if it is a compulsory winding-up: **IA 1986 s.146**) or both (if it is a creditors' voluntary winding-up: **IA 1986 s.106**), to which he shall report on the winding-up.

Within one week of the final meeting prior to dissolution after a voluntary winding-up, the liquidator must send to the Registrar a copy of his accounts and make a return to him of the holding of the meeting; the company is dissolved three months after such registration (**IA 1986 s.201**). In the case of a compulsory winding-up, he must notify the court and the Registrar of the holding and results of the meeting. The company may then be dissolved.

Nevertheless, an application may be made to the court for restoration to the register (**CA 2006 ss.1029–1034**). This will enable the completion of unfinished business, e.g. where a cause of action vested in the company is still outstanding. However, acts done during the period of dissolution will not be validated by the court's order.

STRIKING OFF THE REGISTER

Cheaper than liquidation and formal dissolution is an application to the Registrar for the company to be struck off the register. He may do this if he has reasonable cause to believe that the company is not carrying on business or has been wound up and, after enquiry, no cause is shown why it should not be struck off (**CA 2006 ss.1000–1011**). This procedure will not avail those wishing to deprive members and creditors of the protection afforded to them in liquidation. A company may be restored to the register if at the time of striking off it was carrying on business (so that it should not have been struck off) and it is just to do so (*Re Priceland* (1996)).

MISCONDUCT

Adjustment of Prior Transaction

Where (between the presentation of a petition and the making of an order for administration, or at such other relevant time as is noted below) a company (within two years of the onset of insolvency) has entered into a transaction at an undervalue to the company or given a preference to a person connected with the company or (within six months of the onset of insolvency) has given a preference to a third party, then, on the application of an administrator or liquidator, the court may make an order restoring the position (**IA 1986 ss.238–241**) (see *West Mercia Safetywear v Dodd* (1987)). A preference is caught if (at least partly: *Re Clasper* (1988)) it was influenced by a desire to prefer but not just by a desire to avoid pressure (e.g. calling in of debts: *Re MC Bacon* (1989)). In *Re L Todd* (1989), liability was confined to the amount owed only to creditors intended to be defrauded. The court may also grant relief against extortionate credit transactions entered within three years of an administration order or liquidation (**IA 1986 s.244**).

Wrongful or Fraudulent Trading

It is generally an offence for persons to be involved in trading by a company to defraud creditors (**CA 2006 s.993**). If, during liquidation, it appears that any business of the company has been carried on for any fraudulent purpose, on the application of the liquidator, the court may declare those involved to make such contribution to the company's assets as it thinks proper (**IA 1986 s.213**) to compensate for the loss caused (*Morphitis v Bernasconi* (2002)). Liability under **s.213** may extend to third parties whose knowledge effectively constitutes corporate knowledge, e.g. where they are senior employees or agents and/or the company should have been put on enquiry (*Re BCCI (No.15), Morris v Bank of India* (2005) CA). Dishonesty is an essential ingredient of the offence (*Akt Dansk v Brothers* (2000) HK; *cf. R. v Cox and Hodges* (1982)). But it is sufficient for the fraudulent trading to have occurred on one occasion only (*cf. Re Gerald Cooper* (1978)) and it is unnecessary for action to be taken by the persons defrauded (*R. v Kemp* (1988)).

A director of the company who is aware of impending insolvent liquidation may also be made liable to make such payment as the court thinks proper (**IA 1986 s.214**; *cf. re Continental Assurance (No.4)* (2007)), e.g. the amount by which the company's assets were depleted by the director's misconduct (*Re Produce Marketing Consortium (No.2)* (1989)). Repayment can be ordered to the company but not to individual shareholders (*Re Purpoint* (1990)).

Criminal liability is imposed for certain offences in connection with liquidations (**IA 1986 ss.218 and 432**).

Unfair Prejudice

19

UNDER THE COMPANIES ACTS

As successor to the **CA 1948 s.210** remedy for relief against oppression, **CA 2006 Pt 30 (ss.994–999)** provides a possible alternative remedy to winding-up. In fact, a petition may be brought in the alternative, for winding-up or for unfair prejudice (*Re Garage Door* (1983)), though winding-up on the just and equitable ground may not be possible if relief for unfair prejudice is unavailable (*Re Guidezone* (2000)). (However, companies and members may agree not to exercise the right to apply for the remedy but to refer the matter to arbitration, provided the claim is not for dissolution or to bind third parties: *Fulham FC v Richards* (2010).)

Any member—not merely a person with an expectation of membership (*Re Quickdome* (1988)) or an employee (*Jaber v Science & Information Technology* (1992))—complaining that, by way of any act or omission, the company's affairs are being or would be conducted in a manner unfairly prejudicial to himself and (possibly) other members may petition the court. So may the Secretary of State. Unless their rights are unlikely to be affected and they are "mere investors", all members should be joined in the petition (*Re A Company (No.007281 of 1986)* (1987)). A member may petition though he joined the company aware of the conduct complained of and even though he is using civil proceedings to complain of criminal conduct (*Bermuda Cablevision v Colica* (1997) PC).

The petition must relate to acts done by the company and not by individuals (e.g. by a shareholder exercising his rights as such: *Re Legal Costs* (1999)). Moreover, the remedy is intended to afford relief against conduct which is unfairly prejudicial to "some part of the members" not to all of the members; so, if the alleged prejudice is applied to all shareholders, not discriminating between them, the appropriate remedy is not under **CA 2006 Pt 30** but, more likely, for winding-up on the "just and equitable" ground (*Re A Company (No.00370 of 1987) Ex p. Glossop* (1988)). Also, a petition may be struck out as an abuse of process of the court if alternative means to settle a dispute (e.g. the valuation of the shares of a minority shareholder) already exist (*Re A Company (No.006834 of 1988), ex p. Kremer*, 1988) or if there was no reasonable prospect of a successful petitioner improving his position (e.g. if a reasonable offer was made to buy him out: *Re*

A Co. (No.00836 of 1995) (1996)). It is possible for a majority shareholder to present a petition but it will fail if the petitioner already has the means to resolve the dispute (*Re Legal Costs* (1999)).

The exercise of the remedy depends on the non-fulfilment of the petitioner's contractual rights or legitimate expectations in a way that is unfair (*O'Neill v Phillips* (1999); *Re Guidezone* (2000); *Oak Investment Partners v Boughtwood* (2010) CA). These expectations may be generated during the life of a company, e.g. where a shareholder moves from the position of an employee to a "quasi-partner" (*Croly v Good* (2010)). But the relief will not operate so as to rewrite the terms and understandings upon which the members have become associated (*Re Postgate & Denby* (1986)). Relief against unfair prejudice is not available except for legitimate expectations relating to the conduct of the company's affairs (e.g. not for an unfulfilled expectation that a shareholder would not sell his shares without the consent of the other shareholders: *Re Leeds United Holdings* (1996)) nor simply to fulfil a belief by some members that the company's business will be conducted in a particular way nor an understanding other than between the members. Thus, in *Re Carrington Viyella* (1983), the remedy was not available for past and proposed breaches of an alterable understanding reached between the government and a 49.36 per cent shareholder in the company that, in return for the Government's not making a reference to the Monopolies and Mergers Commission, the shareholder would reduce its voting powers and ultimately its shareholding to 35 per cent. Moreover, mere bad management is a risk which investors must accept (though serious mismanagement such as the managing director's use of company assets for the benefit of his family, thereby diminishing the value of the petitioners shares, is unfairly prejudicial) (*Re Elgindata* (1991)). Where public companies are concerned, the court is unlikely to remedy unfulfilled understandings that are not themselves public (*Re Blue Arrow* (1987)). In a "quasi-partnership" company, operating the company inconsistently with the articles of association may not be unfairly prejudicial if acquiesced in but it will be after the acquiescence ceases (*Fisher v Cadman* (2005)).

If the petition appears well founded, the court may give such relief as it thinks fit. It may: regulate the company's future affairs; require it to take or refrain from taking particular action; order compensation (apparently unrestrained by the reflective loss principle: *Atlasview v Brightview* (2004)); or provide for the purchase of a member's shares (preferring a clean break if a remedy may only temporarily alleviate prejudice: e.g. *Grace v Biagioli* (2005) CA); but it will only entertain a prayer for winding-up as a last resort (*Re A Co. (No.004415 of 1996)* (1997)). If the court's order operates to alter the company's memorandum or articles, no future inconsistent alteration may be made without its leave.

A member may only obtain relief if he (not, e.g. other would-be members whose votes might support his: *Jaber v Science & Information Technology* (1992)) is being oppressed *qua* member. Thus, a petitioner who owned a farm occupied by the company for its business could not *qua* freeholder claim possession of the land in a Pt 30 petition (*Re Cade* (1991)). The mere fact that rights are equally fulfilled does not mean that individual members' interests are. However, mere prejudice, without its being unfair (whether or not that is intended: *Re Sam Weller* (1989)), would be insufficient: e.g. a mere use by the majority of its majority power. So, the drawing by a director who is a majority shareholder of remuneration to which he is not entitled may not be enough, unless he uses his voting strength to procure or retain it or he thereby diminishes the dividends payable to other shareholders (*Irvine v Irvine (No.1)* (2006)). Furthermore, a petition has failed where the articles provided for resolution of disagreement, by one equal participator's being able to remove the other as a director (*Re A Company (No.003096 of 1987)* (1987)). And compelling a member to sell his shares and to leave a quasi-partnership which had broken down, in accordance with the articles, has been held not to be unfairly prejudicial conduct (*Re A Company (No.004377 of 1986)* (1986)). Indeed, a fair offer to buy out the petitioner may defeat the petition (*O'Neill v Phillips* (1999) HL; *cf. Re Benfield Greig Group* (2001): valuation by non-independent valuer).

There is no requirement that the petitioner must come to the court with clean hands but he may be denied relief if his conduct is such that, though he has suffered prejudice, it has not been unfair.

KEY CASE

RE LONDON SCHOOL OF ELECTRONICS (1985)
The petitioner was a director and 25 per cent holder of shares in a tutorial company. The other two directors were the directors and majority shareholders of another company, which held the remaining shares in the company in question. The company was run as a quasi-partnership but the three directors fell out. The petitioner was dismissed as a director, which was publicised in the company's premises; he then discovered that the other directors had been diverting business to the other company, thereby affecting the petitioner's anticipated profits as shareholder. Accordingly, the other company was ordered to purchase his shares, because he had been unfairly prejudiced. The relief and the grounds for it were unaffected by, and not subject to, the fact that, after hearing of the diversion of business, the petitioner had been recruiting amongst the company's students for a new college which he formed (*cf. Grace v Biagioli* (2005) CA).

It is not unfair prejudice for the company not to approve a scheme enabling the sale of shares at an enhanced value, or a scheme for the company to purchase its own shares; or for directors to contemplate using the company's resources to diversify through a subsidiary, for directors must consider using company assets to the best advantage (*Re A Company* (1982)) and may legitimately prefer the interests of the company as a whole to those of a group of shareholders (*Re BSB Holdings (No.2)* (1995)). Similarly, a holding company which receives money as agent of its subsidiary and refuses to pass the money on to its subsidiary may not act to the unfair prejudice of a minority shareholder of the subsidiary if maintenance of the financial health of the group is necessary for the success of the subsidiary (*Nicholas v Soundcraft* (1992)).

Relief is available though a derivative action is possible (it may require restoration to the company: *Clark v Cutland* (2003) CA) and even against an ex-shareholder (e.g. requiring him to purchase the petitioner's shares: *Re A Company* (1986)) or a third party (e.g. if he participated in or benefitted from the action complained of: *Re Little Olympian Each-Ways (No.3)* (1994)). But relief is not available for acts done not by the company but by another shareholder in a personal capacity, e.g. acquiring from a third party an assignment of the company's debt and security (*Re A Company (No.001761 of 1986)* (1986)).

Relief is available on the basis of previous or potential unfair prejudice (e.g. where a majority shareholder summons a meeting which might vote to deprive a minority shareholder of a right of pre-emption: *Re Kenyon Swansea* (1987)). An injunction could even be issued to restrain a rights issue made on favourable terms if it is known that the member could not afford it or it was to deplete the financial resources upon which he was relying to pursue litigation against the company (*Re A Co.* (1984); see also *Re Cumana* (1986)). It may also be available where a director, in breach of his fiduciary duties, sets up a rival company and subordinates his interests in the company to those of the rival (*Re Stewarts* (1981)) or where, in advising on a take-over bid, directors fail to make clear whether they are expressing opinions *qua* shareholders or qua directors (*Re A Co.* (1986)).

Where a majority shareholder enabled another company, in which he was interested, to acquire a major part of an increased shareholding, the court ordered the purchase of a minority shareholding, valued at a date prior to the association with the other company, to avoid any effects of the association (*Re OC Transport* (1984)). On an order for purchase of a minority shareholding, there is no general principle that the price is to be fixed on a valuation *pro rata* with the company's shares as a whole, or with a discount for purchase of a minority shareholding (*Re Bird Precision Bellows* (1985), especially with a "quasi-partnership" (*Strahan v Wilcock* (2006) CA)).

RE BENFIELD SQUASH RACQUETS CLUB (1995)
Directors of a company who were also directors of the majority (86 per cent) shareholder, "FMR", caused the company to grant FMR's bank security over the company's assets, without any possible benefit to the company, and made arrangements for FMR to acquire company assets. Exceptionally, the court ordered FMR to sell its shares to the minority.

UNDER THE INSOLVENCY ACT

An application can be made to the court for relief against unfair prejudice to the interests of a creditor, member or contributory of the company caused by a company voluntary arrangement (see below, pp.117–118) (**IA 1986 s.6(1)(a)**).

On application by a member or creditor, the court may order that an administrator's management of the company's affairs or property is, or has been, unfairly prejudicial to the interest of one or more of them, and grant such relief as it thinks fit: e.g. to regulate the conduct or to discharge the administration order (**IA 1986 s.27**).

Arrangements and Reconstructions

20

GENERAL PROVISION

A company, or certain of its members, may wish for various reasons to alter its capital structure. It may be desired to reduce share capital, because, for example, it is not represented by available assets or it is in excess of the company's needs. A variation of class rights (above, pp.61–62) may be effected for the latter or some other reason. This chapter is primarily concerned with the remaining methods. They may cover arrangements or reconstructions on a purely domestic basis (e.g. paying off certain classes of shareholders or creditors, often debenture-holders) or they may form part of much more ambitious schemes, such as the take-over or merger of two or more companies. The choice of method will often depend on what tax advantages are to be had.

Under the Enterprise Act 2002 Pt 3, the Office of Fair Trading may refer to the Competition Commission for investigation and report where it appears that there is a "relevant merger situation" (i.e., two or more enterprises have ceased or may cease to be distinct enterprises and the value of the enterprise being taken over exceeds £70 million). If the Commission reports that this may be expected to result in a substantial lessening of competition within any market(s) for goods or services, it may recommend action to remedy, mitigate or prevent this.

The ECJ has condemned refusal to recognise the merger of companies of two EU Member States as infringing their rights to freedom of establishment under the EU Treaty (*Re SEVIC Systems* (2005)).

The City Code on Take-overs and Mergers imposes certain standards on take-over bids to ensure adequate disclosure and fair dealings. Its principles are not legally effective but may influence the courts (see *Dunford & Elliott v Johnson & Firth Brown* (1977)). The City Code is issued on the authority of, and administered by, the Panel on Take-overs and Mergers ("the City Panel" or "the Take-over Panel"), the proceedings of which are subject to judicial review (*R. v The Panel on Take-overs and Mergers Ex p. Datafin* (1986)).

1. VARIATION OF CLASS RIGHTS

This may be a necessary preliminary to one of the following schemes. (However, a discharge of rights on a reduction of capital in accordance with the existing rights is not a variation, but a fulfilment of, existing class rights: *House of Fraser v ACGE* (1987)). The procedure is discussed above, in Chapter 12.

2. REDUCTION OF CAPITAL

CA 2006 ss.645–653 provide means whereby a company's capital may be reduced.

If authorised by the articles, a company may by special resolution reduce its share capital. The resolution is ineffective until confirmed by the court and a copy of the court's order and a minute of the company's new structure is registered with the Registrar (*Re Castiglione* (1958)). The words "and reduced" may have to be added to the company's name. Any creditor is *prima facie* entitled to object, so the court should first ensure that all creditors have consented or that their claims have been met or secured. The courts generally only require compliance with the minimum legal requirements.

KEY CASE

CARRUTH V ICI (1937)

It was proposed to reduce the company's capital from £95 million to £89.5 million by cancelling half of the amount of the 10s. deferred shares and then converting four deferred shares into £1 ordinary shares. The scheme was upheld because the variation of the class rights of the deferred shareholders was validly carried out by the class.

In *Scottish Insurance v Wilsons & Clyde* (1949), the company's colliery was nationalised and it was proposed to go into liquidation. The preference shareholders were first validly paid off according to their class rights, with the result that all the compensation for nationalisation accrued to the benefit of the ordinary shareholders (see also *Prudential Assurance v Chatterley-Whitfield* (1949)).

But a reduction which is patently unfair may not be confirmed. In *Re Holder's Investment Trust* (1971), a proposal to cancel cumulative preference shares in exchange for unsecured loan stock was rejected by the court because the majority preference shareholders who secured the passing of the extraordinary resolution of the class were acting in their interests as majority ordinary shareholders rather than as members of the class and the minority had shown the reduction to be unfair.

3. COMPROMISES, ARRANGEMENTS AND RECONSTRUCTIONS

CA 2006 Pt 26 (ss.895–901) provides some control of compromises of disputed claims of the company's creditors and of arrangements modifying the rights of creditors or members, e.g. by dividing shares into different classes or by consolidating shares of different classes. A scheme may be proposed between the company and all of its creditors or members, or a class of either of them. Thus, in formulating a scheme to transfer a group's assets to a new group in which senior lenders would have the bulk of the equity, it was not necessary to consult mezzanine lenders who (because of the group's paucity of assets) had no economic interest in the group and would be shut out (*Re Bluebrook* (2009)). However, the procedure cannot be used to sanction a scheme affecting those with proprietary claims against the company, e.g. under a trust (*Re Lehman Bros International (Europe)* (2009) CA). An arrangement need not alter the rights between the company and its members or creditors (*Re T&N (No.3)* (2006); but, if it does so consistently with the statute, it cannot be attacked by a shareholder as contrary to his human right to non-deprivation of his possessions (*Re Waste Recycling* (2003)).

A member or creditor who is directly affected (or the liquidator, if the company is being wound up) may apply to the court, which can order a meeting of the class affected. The notice of such a meeting must explain the effect of the scheme and, especially, its effect on the interests of any directors or trustees for debenture-holders concerned.

The scheme will be effective if:

(a) it is voted for by three-fourths in value of those present at the meeting and entitled to vote;

(b) the court sanctions the scheme (which it can only do if the company has approved it: *Re Savoy Hotel* (1981)); and

(c) the Registrar receives a copy of the court's order.

In deciding whether to sanction the scheme, the court must first ensure that the correct procedure has been followed. Once it is satisfied of that, it will generally assume that the scheme is fair, having been passed by the majority. But it may decline to sanction it if an objective reasonably intelligent member of the class, acting from its own interests, might not approve.

KEY CASE

RE HELLENIC & GENERAL TRUST (1975)
It was proposed to cancel the ordinary shares of Hellenic and to issue new ones to Hambros, thus making it a wholly owned subsidiary of Hambros. The price offered for the shares by Hambros was fair but NBG (which owned 14 per cent of them) would become liable to pay heavy capital gains tax in Greece. The scheme received the necessary majority but was not sanctioned by the court because the class meeting voting for it was held to be improperly constituted, as it included a share-holder (MIT, with 41 per cent of the shares) which was already a wholly owned subsidiary of Hambros and so, it was said, a separate class!

Where the whole or part of a company's undertaking or property is to be transferred to another company, the court has additional powers to facilitate the transfer: e.g. to allot securities in the original company to the other one.

Where **CA 2006 Pt 26** is being used for the merger or division of a public limited company, in consideration for shares in the transferee company or companies, then in specified cases the transaction is ineffective unless sanctioned by at least three-fourths in value of the votes cast of each class of members of every pre-existing transferee company concerned (**CA 2006 Pt 27**).

. . . .

4. ACQUISITION OF MEMBERS' SHARES

In general, if shares are freely transferable, they can be easily purchased by any person (whether an individual or a corporation) who wishes to do so. Such a person who intends to acquire sufficient shares to enable him to obtain control of the company is considered to be making a "take-over bid". Subject to the usual freedoms and restrictions on contracting for the pur-chase of shares, he is free to do so, though he should comply with the City Code.

CA 2006 Pt 28, Ch.3 (ss.974–991) provides a means whereby minority shareholdings can be acquired by the transferor and sold by the minority.

Where a person, making a take-over offer on the same terms for all the shares of a company or of a class of shares (**CA 2006 s.974**), has acquired or contracted to acquire at least nine-tenths in value of the relevant shares, he may give notice to the holder of any remaining such shares that he desires to acquire those shares (**CA 2006 s.979**). He then becomes prima facie entitled to acquire those shares on the same terms on which the shares of the other shareholders are to be transferred, and for those shareholders to be "squeezed out" from the company.

KEY CASE

RE CARLTON HOLDINGS (1971)
Underwriters, on behalf of the transferee company, made an original offer to shareholders in the transferor company of either shares in the transferee company or a cash sum (from the underwriters). When the transferee company later came to exercise its rights under the sections, it had to offer the same terms to the minority, so that they could opt for the cash alternative.

Dissenting minority shareholders have a right, within six weeks of notice of the intention to acquire their shares, to apply to the court, which may order that the acquisition shall be on such terms as it thinks fit (**CA 2006 s.986**). Thus, objection may be made where the 90 per cent holding was acquired by the transferee company as a result of the accepting shareholders' being misled (*Gething v Kilner* (1971)) or where the scheme is unfair to the shareholders as a body, and not merely to individual shareholders (*Re Grierson* (1968)).

KEY CASE

RE BUGLE PRESS (1961)
The majority shareholders in one company formed a second company to which they transferred their shares so that the second company could acquire the shares of the minority in the original company. The court would not let the Act be used for the purpose of getting rid of an unwanted minority in this way.

A shareholder may require the acquirer of a 90 per cent shareholding to buy out his shares on similar terms (a "sell-out") (**CA 2006 s.983**).

5. ARRANGEMENTS

To avoid the complications of the procedure under **CA 2006 Pt 26** (above, pp.115–116), **IA 1986 ss.1–7** affords a simple procedure whereby a company may conclude with its creditors a composition in satisfaction of its debts or a scheme of arrangement of its affairs.

Where the directors of an eligible company propose a voluntary arrangement, they may apply to the court for a moratorium (**IA 1986 s.1A**). While in force, a moratorium restricts petitions to wind up, company meetings, resolutions to wind up, appointment of administrative receivers, and the enforcement of security over company property and other proceedings against the company (**IA 1986 Sch.1A**).

A proposal for a voluntary arrangement may be made by:

(a) the directors, or

(b) the administrator, if the company is in administration, or

(c) during winding-up, the liquidator.

The proposal must provide for a nominee (who must be an insolvency practitioner or authorised nominee) to act as trustee or otherwise for the purpose of supervising its implementation (**IA 1986 s.1**).

(After a report to the court, where the nominee is not an administrator or liquidator: **IA 1986 s.2**) the nominee should summon meetings of the company and of its creditors (**IA 1986 s.3**), which can decide (subject to safeguarding the rights of secured and preferential creditors) whether to approve the proposed voluntary arrangement (with or without modifications) (**IA 1986 s.4**). If approved, it binds the company and every person entitled to be present at the meeting, and the court may facilitate implementation of the arrangement in preference to any current administration or winding-up (**IA 1986 s.5**).

On the application of a person entitled to vote at the meetings, the nominee or (during administration or winding-up) the administrator or liquidator, the court may revoke the approval(s) of the arrangement or direct reconsideration at further meetings if:

(a) the approved voluntary arrangement unfairly prejudices the interest of a creditor, member or contributor of the company, or

(b) there has been some material irregularity with respect to the meetings (**IA 1986 s.6**).

The court has supervisory jurisdiction over the person who is the supervisor of an approved voluntary arrangement (**IA 1986 s.7**).

6. ARRANGEMENTS BY LIQUIDATORS

In a voluntary liquidation, where it is proposed to sell or transfer the whole or part of a company's undertaking or property to another ("transferee") company, the liquidator may, if authorised by special resolution (in a members' voluntary winding-up) or the sanction of the court or the liquidation committee (in a creditor's voluntary winding-up), receive as part or whole of the consideration shares or other interests in the transferee company, or he may enter into an arrangement whereby the members may, in addition to or in lieu of receiving such interests, receive other benefits from the transferee company (**IA 1986 s.110**).

The liquidator is otherwise bound by the rules governing voluntary liquidations and must accord creditors and members their normal rights: e.g. members' rights to participate in the consideration received depend on their rights in such liquidations (*Griffith v Paget* (1877)). Any member who dissents from the proposal may, within seven days, require the liquidator in writing not to proceed or to purchase his interests before proceeding (**IA 1986 s.111**), and the company's constitution cannot take away this right (*Bisgood v Henderson's Transvaal Estates* (1908)).

The court is not required to sanction the scheme and will only be involved if a member applies to it to have his rights upheld or if an application is made for compulsory liquidation; the latter may be done within a year of the special resolution, which will then be void unless sanctioned by the court. Otherwise, any sale or agreement under **IA 1986 s.110** binds all members and creditors.

If a scheme which comes within the terms of **IA 1986 s.110** cannot be carried out (e.g. because the necessary resolution fails), the court may sanction it under **CA 2006 Pt 26** (above, pp.115–116), although, if it does, it can require that dissentients receive the protection they would do under **IA 1986 s.110** (*Re Anglo-Continental Supply* (1922)). However, it was held in *Re General Motor Cab* (1913) that, if the scheme is really a sale, then **IA 1986 s.110** must be used, not **CA 1985 s.425**. The case is generally assumed to be weak authority but it was treated as correct in *Re Hellenic* (above, p.116).

. . . .
7. OTHER COMPROMISES AND ARRANGEMENTS IN LIQUIDATION

With the sanction of:
(a) the court or the liquidation committee in a compulsory liquidation (**IA 1986 s.167**), or
(b) an extraordinary resolution of the company in a members' voluntary liquidation (**IA 1986 s.165**), or
(c) the court, the liquidation committee or a meeting of creditors in a creditors' voluntary liquidation (**IA 1986 s.165**), the liquidator may enter into any compromise or arrangement with creditors.

In doing so, the liquidator can exercise the powers listed in **IA 1986 Sch.4**, some of which are not exercisable without sanction.

The liquidator cannot exercise his powers under **IA 1986 s.165** to distribute assets other than according to the creditors' rights; **CA 2006 Pt 26** (above, pp.115–116) must be used, under which dissenting creditors have a right to object (*Re Trix* (1970)).

Examination Checklist

NB These questions generally follow the order in which the topics appear in this book. But not all of them do. In particular, some cannot be answered fully without looking at material discussed in more than one chapter.

1   In which ways may persons carry on or become involved in business activities?

2   Distinguish between different types of companies.

3   What are the requirements for setting up a registered company?

4   What is a promoter? In what ways may he incur liability, and to whom?

5   What are the legal consequences of pre-incorporation contracts?

6   What is the legal liability of someone who induces, or attempts to induce, others to invest in limited companies?

7   In what ways can companies raise finance?

8   What is capital? What are the different types of capital?

9   What is maintenance of capital? How is it achieved?

10   In what ways can company money be paid out?

11   What does it mean that a person is a shareholder? How does (s)he become one? How does (s)he cease to be one?

12   What is insider dealing? What is wrong with it? How can it be justified? What are the consequences of market abuse?

13   What is a debenture? Compare the position of a debenture-holder with a shareholder.

14   What is a charge? What is the difference between a fixed and a floating charge? When are charges (not) effective?

15   What is a retention of title clause? When is it effective?

16   What are the rules governing priority between different claimants?

17   What is corporate personality? What are its advantages and disadvantages? How can it be circumvented?

18   To what extent is the capacity of a company different from that of an individual?

19   In what circumstances is a company liable for those who do acts affecting it?

20   To what extent is a company liable for crimes and torts committed in respect of its activities?

21   What is the significance of a company's memorandum and articles of association?

22 What are class rights? How can they be varied?

23 What is corporate governance? How are companies run?

24 What are the general meeting and the board of directors, and what is the relationship between them?

25 What role or rights do, or should, employees have in the operation of companies?

26 What is a director? Who can, and cannot, be a director?

27 What are the duties and the rights of directors?

28 What are receivers, administrators and liquidators? What are their rights and duties?

29 What is administration?

30 How are decisions made as to how companies should be run?

31 What is the importance of majority rule? How is it balanced with the rights of individuals and minorities? What is the rule in *Foss v Harbottle*? What is a derivative action? What is fraud on the minority?

32 What external control is there over the way company affairs are conducted?

33 What is insolvency? What is its effect on running a company?

34 What are liquidation and winding-up? When can they occur?

35 In what ways can a person be held liable to account for misconduct in activities connected with a company?

36 What is the purpose of the remedy against unfair prejudice? How does it operate? Is it working successfully?

37 What are arrangements and reconstructions? What is the point of them? How can they be affected?

Sample Questions and Model Answers

....

PREPARATION

For those using this book simply as a revision text, it will probably be too late to take full advantage of the points about basic preparation for an examination—albeit some use may still be made of them. For those also using the book as an introductory text, some very basic points can usefully be borne in mind.

The first and most obvious is that, whether the course of study has an academic or a practical bias (and ideally, the student should have regard to both—to know how the law works in the real world and to understand the theories lying behind it), preparation for the examination begins at the beginning of the course. A student who has not worked diligently and steadily through the material (and, whatever parts of the subject may be omitted from the syllabus being followed, there is a great deal of material in Company Law) will have inadequate familiarity with the rules and inadequate appreciation of the practical circumstances in which they operate. The necessary reservoir of knowledge and experience (even when many of the details have been forgotten) cannot be assimilated during last minute revision. So, all the work set should be done at the proper time and orderly and intelligible notes prepared.

This is particularly important in Company Law because, as a glance at the main textbooks reveals, the presentation of the rather complex and voluminous material does not follow as consistent a pattern as in many other areas of the law. Students should always accept that no reading list is by any means a perfect guide to the material, that further reading may be necessary to amplify a particular subject or simply to check up points which are unexplained or insufficiently explained in the basic reading material. But further reference is considerably hindered by an initially inadequate grounding.

Some further points need to be stressed in this context. Depending upon the conventions of the course and the practices of the examination board (which must not be assumed never to change), candidates tend to concentrate their revision on particular areas, whether because they enjoyed studying these subjects, they are central subjects which regularly appear on the examination paper, or they deal with particularly significant recent developments (which often, though not always, appeal to examiners looking for new ideas for questions or to see how up-to-date the candidate's knowledge and understanding is). It is not easy to recognise the relevant areas without a thorough grounding in the whole syllabus, and it can be devastating to discover this for the first time when reading the question paper and fatal to answer all or part of a question wrongly or completely off the point for having failed to realise what it is really about. Furthermore, there is never any guarantee that an indication of the correct area(s) is given by the order in which subjects usually appear on the examination paper or, more importantly, that a question on a favourite topic will not incorporate one or more points from an unpopular one. Depending upon his or her impression of the paper as a whole, a candidate might feel it worthwhile to answer such a question regardless. But he or she should be in a position to make an informed judgment and, ideally, have a sufficient (even if only fairly rudimentary) knowledge of the other area(s) to enhance the answer and the marks available.

By the end of the course of study, students should know, and should make certain they know exactly, with what areas they are expected to be familiar, what emphasis on different aspects may be imposed by the examiners and, if this can be ascertained, what sort of approach is expected by the examiners, in particular whether it is very practical or theoretical, and so on.

REVISION

Different people revise in different ways, so this is largely a matter of personal taste. One obvious goal, however, is to ensure that adequate time is available. It is sensible to draw up a time-table in advance, with sufficient flexibility to allow for different rates of progress as well as unwelcome interruptions. It is particularly important to ensure that the coursework has been completed before the revision period, so that there is no unfinished reading left either to be done or to be abandoned.

A review of recent past papers can be invaluable, so long as they are not read obsessively and in the expectation of their providing an accurate guide to the examination impending. Even more valuable is practice in answering papers under examination conditions—and, if possible, to have the answers marked by examiners or teachers. This is usually assumed to be fairly obvious but something which can be postponed so as not to intrude on revision time or for other reasons. This is a mistake often born of a certain amount of cowardice. Practice with answering questions throws into relief how questions are designed, how good candidates are at planning and constructing answers in the time given, how much knowledge candidates do and do not have, and how that knowledge can or should be employed in answering the questions set. Perhaps most important (and, despite the time occupied in attempting mock answers, most useful in terms of rendering revision efficient) is the instruction obtained as to how little that can in reality be written in the time available for each question. An enormous amount of detailed knowledge will be found to be useless if the candidate does not have a sound understanding of the basic elements, structure and materials of the subject. Once that is grasped, more detailed knowledge can be employed to deepen understanding and to provide a body of material on which to draw. A few practice papers can develop considerably the necessary techniques to do well in the examination.

It can be particularly instructive to compare answers with friends. Most candidates only know their own style and are uncertain as to what they are doing right and what they are doing wrong. Reading through a variety of answers can be very revealing as to techniques which might be adopted or discarded.

THE EXAMINATION

It should go without saying that the whole of the question paper should be read carefully not only to elucidate the contents of the individual questions but to get quite clear what is generally being required. The examiner has decided how many questions need to be answered, if there are any compulsory questions, if a certain number of problems and/or essays must be answered, and if questions must be selected from particular sections. If there are such requirements, it is up to the candidate to satisfy them and not to present a script which has not been demanded. Normally there is some choice, and usually there is no requirement for questions to be answered in a particular order. But candidates must at all times do what they are told!

The last injunction extends to the particular directions issued in each question. Most problem questions ask the candidate to "Advise X." So, do so. Probably most of the question is concerned with more general matters: Is the transaction valid? Is there a breach of an obligation? And so on. And most of the marks will be gained in dealing with these matters. But it frequently takes little effort or additional knowledge actually to advise X. Should he sue for damages or specific performance, bring a derivative action, petition for winding-up or for unfair prejudice, sell his shares, or be able to do these things but without its in fact being worth his while to do so. Set out the legal position and the possible remedies, and then give advice which suits X in the circumstances. To do this whilst writing mock answers helps to concentrate the mind as to how the law operates in practical circumstances.

Similarly, with essay questions. An older generation of teachers may still refer to these as "bookwork questions," the assumption being that they are set for the weaker candidates, unable to acquit themselves adequately on problem questions, who can at least, therefore, trot out a certain amount of knowledge on a general topic and pick up a few marks. Traces of this view do occasionally persist. More frequently at present, however, candidates are expected to demonstrate analytical and critical skills. So "discuss" means "discuss" and not "write what you know about". This is not necessarily as demanding as it seems. A question requiring the candidate to discuss the extent to which a particular statement is or is not true will generally require the presentation of the information which would be provided if the candidate were simply required to write all he knows: where marks can be gained in an essay question is to do this with explicit reference to the question. It does not usually require much intelligence to link the facts with the demands of the question.

Timing

The question paper may indicate that more time should be spent on some parts than others (e.g. where certain questions carry a larger proportion of the overall marks). Usually, it can be presumed that an equal amount of time is to be devoted to each question. It is not uncommon for a little more time to be spent on a candidate's first (and expected best) question and a little less on the last question (when the race against time may increase the speed at which the words hit the page). But there should not be much deviation from the principle of equality. It is not very difficult to pick up a minimum amount of marks for a question but examiners tend to be more cautious higher up the scale. And in practice the difference between poor marks and good marks may not be great. Assume a grading system for a degree where the marks per class are for: a pass, 40; a third, 45; a lower second, 50; an upper second, 60; and a first, 70. On a paper requiring four questions to be answered, this works out at 10, 11.25, 12.5, 15 and 17.5 for individual questions. Assume the marks of the majority of candidates fall between 38 and 72 per cent. A not very strong candidate or an average candidate for some reason or other not performing very well on the day might amass, say, an average of 13 marks per question, which produces 52, a lower second class (even if not an especially good one). If that candidate (still performing generally below average) put in a special effort on his first three questions and left little time for the fourth, he might get marks of 16, 14, 13 and 4, i.e. a total of 47 per cent and a degree of the next class down. An even weaker candidate could succeed in failing! It is better to build up a sound overall foundation of marks for each and every question before taking chances.

Planning the Answer

Different teachers may give different advice on this. Candidates may consider varying the response depending upon whether the adviser is marking the paper, although that should not make a difference.

It is at least sensible to jot down briefly the points to be made and the order in which they should be made (plus the names of relevant authorities, lest they are forgotten). Some examiners like to see an introduction plus an outline of what is to be discussed. However, this may be a waste of time, particularly if the candidate is tempted just to waffle an introduction while he is waiting for his mind to start working. Don't ever waste time! It runs out soon enough. It is often best simply to get on with the answer.

In a problem, it is usually most convenient to take the points as they arise in the question. Conclusions should be brief and to the point and not simply repeat what has already been said (especially as it might be contradicted!). Conclusions should also—obviously!—appear at the end. It is not uncommon for a person answering an essay question to begin by agreeing with a quotation and then to proceed to find fault with it. Summarise at the end what you do think, not at the beginning what you hope you might think.

It can be helpful in answering both essay and problem questions to think in terms of discharging the functions of a barrister arguing in court, an academic writing a learned article, a judge giving judgment and a solicitor advising his client. Consider both sides of a point, offer some criticism of the merits of the relevant law, then come to a conclusion of the law and how that can dictate action.

All the time, however, follow the instructions in the question paper. It is not enough to try to impress the examiner with what you could do if that is not what is required. By setting a limited number of answers, the examiner is taking a sample of your general competence throughout the whole of Company Law. But you must give him the sample he asks for, not something different. Moreover, you are expected to show an ability to discriminate between the relevant and the irrelevant.

Information

However academic your answer may be, it must be as much supported by relevant information as the most practical of answers. So don't allow your attempts to show how clever you are to lead you to omit any of the relevant knowledge which you can usefully demonstrate. Always cite relevant authorities—and underlining them highlights them. Don't regurgitate more facts than are necessary; though try succinctly to give an indication of the precise relevance of the authorities to the points in the question.

Never assume that you can acquire information in the examination room. It is a common practice to allow candidates to have a collection of statutes with them. (If you must provide these yourself, make sure you get the approved edition well before the shops are sold out, and find out if you are permitted to make any marks, of any description, in the book. If in doubt, make sure there are no such marks—otherwise you may commit an examination offence and fail the examination.) If you are not familiar with such materials before the examination, it is too late to attempt familiarity in the examination room, when you are under pressure and probably will not be able to find something even if you have a rough idea of where to look. This is especially so where the legislation is very complex, as it is in Company Law. Such materials can only be relied upon to verify points which you have already learnt but where the precise detail has escaped you.

METHOD OF ANSWERING QUESTIONS

There is no such thing as a perfect answer: a degree candidate usually only needs 70 per cent for a first class mark (difficult though that may be to achieve). And, surprising as it may seem, examiners are human beings with inevitably varying preferences and prejudices. Nonetheless, the job of marking produces remarkably consistent results whoever the examiner is. The trick is to present an informed, well reasoned and intelligent argument. The following two sections give some indication of the sort of approach required.

ESSAY QUESTION

Example

> "The rule in *Salomon v A. Salomon & Co. Ltd* can truly be said to be a cornerstone of English Company Law."
> Do you agree?

Preliminary

Like many essay questions, this can be answered in different ways. You should begin, however, by giving some thought as to the proposed structure of your answer and to giving a balanced and reasoned approach which is not limited to either simply trotting out your notes on corporate personality or slavish adherence to the words of the question.

Don't begin by copying out the question—the examiner knows that he has asked you and will not give you any credit for demonstrating your inability to realise that you are wasting your time.

You should not assume that the statement is correct and that the examiner expects you to agree with it or that, if you do not think that it is entirely true, then it must be entirely wrong. Think of what position you expect to take and try to be consistent in your answer. But you should always balance your view with any possible opposing views and be ready to take on the fact that, as the adrenalin flows and your mind concentrates on the question you are answering, you may form a somewhat different view from the one with which you began. So don't begin by saying "I think that it is generally true that ...". You should present your case in an informative and balanced way before reaching your conclusion, especially because you should be arguing from the law, as it stands and as it should be, rather than simply from what you personally might happen to think. Some examiners prefer candidates' views to be expressed in terms of impartial submissions ("therefore, it is submitted that" and so on). This is not compulsory and might be thought to betray an overly pedantic imitation of the language of the barrister in court. But it can be useful in reminding you that you cannot legitimately argue about the law without first demonstrating what the law is and that, for your arguments to be acceptable, they should be based upon your understanding and presentation of that law before you go on to criticise the law more radically.

The Answer

If there were nothing unusual about *Salomon*, it would be unlikely to attract so much attention. Therefore, it can be useful to begin by outlining the "normal" situation. A natural person who engages in trade is not only entitled to the advantages of the rights possessed by other natural persons. He is subject to disadvantages. Quite apart from the fact it is inconvenient to trade without some association with others, his personal finances are likely to be limited and he may find it difficult to increase them by borrowing by means of simple (unsecured?) loans which have to be repaid, and repaid with interest. In particular, if he should incur liabilities, they may considerably exceed any means he has or can acquire to satisfy them.

Parliament has, therefore, provided for trading by means of companies with limited liability. Although candidates should normally only make minimal reference to the facts of cases, the centrality of *Salomon* itself is so obvious that a brief outline of the facts of the case and of the precise *ratio decidendi* should be given. Then, consider whether on the facts of *Salomon* the decision appears to be just and sensible. Was *Salomon*'s company the sort which the legislation had in mind? Was he abusing the privileges granted by statute? Did the House of Lords simply give effect to the words of the statute without wishing to interpret them in a "realistic" way? And so on.

Next consider with reference to the authorities the circumstances in which *Salomon* has been applied, the advantages and disadvantages of the rule (from the point of view of those actively engaged in running the company, mere investors and third parties dealing with the company). Note especially any area in which the court may have appeared inconsistent or to have shifted direction, e.g. in the insurance cases *Macaura, Wilson v Jones, Kosmopoulos* (not an English case—mention in such a situation how you think an English court would respond to it) and *The Moonacre*.

This part of the discussion can also profitably tie in with a review of the principal elements of Company Law generally. Always remember what the question says. It does not simply ask about the *Salomon* case. It expects it to be considered in the context of English Company Law in general. So, briefly, how does *Salomon* tie up with other areas, if at all, e.g. in relation to the participation of shareholders in corporate decision making.

The functioning of the corporate person can here be examined from the point of view of the character of the corporate person—in what respects it is treated in the same way and, in particular, differently from natural persons: e.g. how is its "directing mind and will" identified?

Having assessed the position in relation to the identity and operation of the corporate person, special attention must be devoted to situations in which the veil is lifted. This can be done fairly easily by presenting a list of "exceptions" to the general position and noting the circumstances of the relevant cases. Whereas a demonstration of knowledge will amass some marks, this should be presented in terms of principles governing, and reasons for, the "exceptional" cases and especially whether they are simply exceptions or in some way compatible with the general doctrine.

Finally, summarise the status of *Salomon* in relation to the specific thrust of the question set. You are not required simply to agree or disagree. Thus, if you decide that, all things considered, it is a cornerstone, you do not need to conclude that it is the only or most important one.

. . . .

PROBLEM QUESTIONS

The Question
Slimber Plc carries on a varied timber processing business. Pinto Ltd regularly supplies it with pine logs, some of which Slimber uses in the manufacture of furniture, the less suitable parts of which it cuts into stakes to be sold for fencing. Pinto supplies the logs under contracts providing that ownership of all wood supplied to Slimber and its products shall remain in Pinto and all

moneys received for the sale of such wood and products held on trust for Pinto exclusively until all debts due from Slimber to Pinto have been discharged. David (the brother of Edwin, the managing director of Slimber) regularly supplies Slimber with metal rods, which Slimber uses to strengthen items of furniture manufactured by it.

Five months ago, Rory, a retailer and purchaser of furniture from Slimber, obtained judgment against Slimber for £50,000 damages for losses suffered by Rory in consequence of furniture supplied to Rory by Slimber, the furniture being defective because some of the rods in it were corroded. In order to pay the damages, Slimber needs to increase its profits but David refuses to continue supplying steel rods unless Slimber pays £5,000 for rods already supplied and pays in advance for future deliveries, which Slimber is unable to do. While Edwin and his secretary, Freda, are on holiday, another of Slimber's directors, George, persuades David to continue supplies if Slimber grants David a fixed charge over its sawmill for moneys owed up to £20,000.

However, the news of Rory's action against Slimber causes its trade to dwindle. In the last six months, none of the directors or their secretaries have been paid nor has the annual dividend, declared three months ago. A creditor petitions for compulsory winding-up and a liquidator is appointed.

Advise the liquidator.

The Answer
First, outline the duties and powers of a liquidator. Extensive discussion of these is not required on the facts but they form the background of your advice. See generally IA 1986 ss.165–168. Clearly, he should discharge the duty of a liquidator in a compulsory winding-up if assuming control of company property (IA 1986 s.144). Presumably, he will wish to realise the companies assets (how? does he require sanction?). Are there any particular powers he may wish to exercise in this respect? If Slimber were held liable to Rory because of defective rods in the furniture, might not David in turn be liable to Slimber for having supplied defective rods to Slimber? Don't automatically say that the liquidator should sue David: it might have been Slimber's fault if they left the rods out in the rain and they rusted; possibly David will agree that it was his fault and will pay up if he is asked, without the liquidator's having to spend time and money suing him; similarly, if Slimber owes money to David, the liquidator can save time and money by simply setting-off from the debt any money claimed from David. The liquidator should wind up the company as efficiently and economically as possible. Give him good practical advice.

Once the financial situation is reasonably clear, the next obvious step is to pay the creditors (some are mentioned in the question; there may be others). Presumably the company is insolvent, in which case it is not a simple case of paying all creditors in full. Note that it may be advantageous to make compromises or arrangements with creditors. Can the liquidator exercise powers in these respects without sanction? If sanction is required, whose? In realising the company's assets and deciding on the priority of claimants, it will be necessary to defer to the valid claims of secured creditors.

First, consider Pinto. He has supplied goods under a retention of title clause. What are the objects of such clauses and what conditions must be met to secure those objects: see *Aluminium v Romalpa*. What are the objections to such clauses? When are they likely to fail to have the desired effect? If potentially ineffectual, can they be made effectual (e.g. by registration)? What is the effect of registration? See *Re Bond Worth*. What are the consequences of Pinto's clause being held effective (see also *Clough Mill v Martin*)? What if the clause is ineffective? Does Pinto recover nothing or just have a personal claim? If the latter, where does he come in order of priority? Does the clause have different effects in relation to: unused logs; logs cut into stakes; logs cut and incorporated into furniture; the proceeds of sale?

What of David's fixed charge? In what circumstances is this normally valid? Does it need registration? If valid, what is its effect? If invalid, what of David's claims? Whatever the normal position, does the giving of it by the company to David at the relevant time constitute a preference? See IA 1986 ss.239–240. If so, what are the consequences for the charge of any claims David might have?

Having ascertained whether or not there are claimants with proprietory or security rights which they can enforce, in what order are the remaining claims to be paid? First, there are the expenses of winding-up. Next, the preferential payments listed by IA 1986 ss.175, 386 and Sch.6. Clearly, there is a claim for remuneration of employees (are directors employees?) and this includes at least one claim for holiday remuneration (Freda's). If the company has been having difficulties there will probably be other creditors entitled to preference—these can be mentioned in outline. Are these preferential creditors to be paid in any particular order or pari passu (what does pari passu mean?)? Note the different periods for the preferential debts. Are there any parts of such debts outside the preferred period? What is the effect of being outside the period?

Next the unsecured creditors' fund must be dealt with. After that, the claims of debenture-holders with floating charges (if any) are payable and then all other debts provable in bankruptcy (which includes all debts or parts of debts without higher ranking, such as Rory's judgment for damages, if not previously satisfied). These are payable *pari passu*—relevant again if the assets are insufficient.

Any remaining assets are distributed in accordance with the members' rights on liquidation. Maybe there are none left, but not necessarily—the fact that there was insufficient available cash before liquidation does not mean there may not be a surplus once the assets are realised.

Finally, to round off, the liquidator should call and present his report to a final meeting of the creditors (IA 1986 s.146), of which he must notify the court and the Registrar, to whom he must make a return and supply a copy of his accounts.

. . . .

FINALLY

Good luck!

Index

This index has been prepared using Sweet and Maxwell's Legal Taxonomy. Main index entries conform to keywords provided by the Legal Taxonomy except where references to specific documents or non-standard terms (denoted by quotation marks) have been included. These keywords provide a means of identifying similar concepts in other Sweet and Maxwell publications and on-line services to which keywords from the Legal Taxonomy have been applied. Readers may find some differences between terms used in the text and those which appear in the index.